I0797569

Twelve Years with Hitler

Christa Schroeder at her typewriter in
Führer HQ Wolfsschanze

TWELVE YEARS WITH HITLER

Secretary to the Führer

Albert Zoller – Christa Schroeder

Foreword by Roger Moorhouse

Translated by Heather Williams

Greenhill Books

Twelve Years with Hitler

Greenhill Books

First French edition: *Douze ans auprès d'Hitler, confidences d'une secrétaire particulière d'Hitler* by Albert Zoller, René Julliard, 1949
Librairie Arthème Fayard, 1952

First published by Greenhill Books, 2025
Greenhill Books, c/o Pen & Sword Books Ltd,
George House, Unit 12 & 13, Beevor Street, Off Pontefract Road,
Barnsley, South Yorkshire S71 1HN

For more information on our books, please visit
www.greenhillbooks.com, email contact@greenhillbooks.com
or write to us at the above address.

CIP data records for this title are available from the British Library

ISBN 978-1-8050-0134-8

Typeset in 12.5/18pt Adobe Caslon Pro by JCS Publishing Services Ltd
Printed and bound in Great Britain by CPI Group (UK) Ltd, Croydon CR10 4YY

CONTENTS

FOREWORD
by Roger Moorhouse

Emilie Christine Schroeder was born in Hannoversch Münden in Lower Saxony in 1908. Coming from a lower-middle-class family and orphaned as a teenager, she trained as a typist to make ends meet. It was a decision that would change her life.

After replying to a classified advertisement, she took a job at the headquarters of the Sturmabteilung, or SA – Hitler's 'Brownshirts' – in 1930. And, three years later, she came to the attention of Hitler himself, when she was brought in to deputise for his usual secretary – one Herta Frey – for urgent dictation. She would work for Hitler, very closely, on call twenty-four hours a day, for the next twelve years, accompanying the Führer on all his travels, to the Berghof in Bavaria, to the 'Wolf's Lair' in East Prussia and to the Reich Chancellery in Berlin, where she would be one of the last to leave the bunker, shortly before Hitler's suicide on 30 April 1945.

As might have been expected, given her erstwhile proximity to Hitler, Schroeder was arrested by the Americans at the end of the war and was produced as a prosecution witness at the Nuremberg Tribunal. After that, she was interned in a succession of camps and prisons, and subjected to extensive interrogation, before being tried, convicted and then cleared of criminal cooperation with the

Nazi regime. She was released in 1948 and returned to working as a secretary.

History would not be so easy for Schroeder to leave behind, however. The year after her release, an account of her interrogations appeared, in serialised form, in the popular French magazine *Constellation*. Shortly after the war, she had been interrogated in an internment camp in Augsburg by a French Army captain, Albert Bernhard – who later used the alias Albert Zoller – who had gained her trust and persuaded her to provide him with extensive notes on her memories and reflections on her time with Hitler. It was those reminiscences that were now doing the rounds under Zoller's name, and which duly appeared under the title *Douze ans auprès d'Hitler, confidences d'une secrétaire particulière d'Hitler*, or in German as *Hitler Privat*, in 1949.

For his part, Zoller had also interviewed Hermann Göring in Nuremberg, and had corresponded with Schroeder about the possibility of issuing the book under joint authorship, but the discussions came to nothing. It may be that Schroeder was keen to move on from her past, or that she was then still unwilling to compromise others from that chapter in her life who were still alive. It may also be that she felt that the relationship that she had had with Zoller – and it is not entirely clear what precise form it had taken – had been betrayed by the publication, and she wanted nothing more to do with him. Whatever the reason, her name did not appear on the cover of the book, despite most of it – by her estimate around 70 per cent – consisting of material that she had provided.

Later in her life, Schroeder would collaborate with the German historian Anton Joachimsthaler, in compiling another account of her life, which on her insistence would be published posthumously, and duly appeared – under her name this time – the year after her death in Munich in 1984, with the title: *Er war Mein Chef.* This book was published in translation by Frontline, with an introduction by me, in 2009 as *He Was My Chief: The Memoirs of Hitler's Secretary.*

So, what then of this volume? The narrative of Schroeder's career proceeds broadly chronologically, through sixteen chapters, each one dealing with a specific period as well as a theme, such as Hitler's relationship with women, or his routines when at his various headquarters. Reading it today, one is struck first of all by Schroeder's tone. She comes across throughout as erudite and objective: a woman fully aware of the significance of the world through which she was moving, with all its benefits, hypocrisies and absurdities. She is a very competent and sure-footed guide to the rarified upper echelons of the Third Reich, and she does not hold back with her opinions. She is certainly no starry-eyed ingenue. She describes Eva Braun, for instance, as a 'dull little courtesan', while Martin Bormann managed to be simultaneously 'a bit dense' and 'an evil genius'.

Hitler, too, does not escape criticism. Though Schroeder remembered him from the early years as a surprisingly caring and compassionate figure, a man with 'magnetic radiance' – and with the famously Viennese manner of kissing ladies' hands – her view of him changed somewhat over time. By the closing months of the war, for example, she described him as 'a monster of cruelty' and a 'tyrant', not only for his behaviour to her personally – he turned on her after she publicly contradicted him – but also for his brutal treatment of his opponents. Nonetheless, one senses that those criticisms were rather tempered by her admiration for and loyalty to the man whom she called her '*Chef*'.

One aspect that is perhaps lacking in this book is an appreciation on Schroeder's behalf of the broader events of the period. Despite her evident ability and intelligence, one searches her account in vain for all but the briefest reference to the wider war, for instance, or to the Holocaust. Some have interpreted this as a desire to whitewash those events, to wish them away in favour of a sanitised presentation of the Third Reich almost as a kitchen-sink drama, a world of receptions and exotic headquarters, and late-night dictation. There may be something in that, of course, but I think that the truth is probably rather more prosaic. Schroeder was recalling events as she saw them; her perspective – for all that proximity to the very epicentre of Nazi power – was necessarily limited. She would not have been party to sensitive discussions of racial policy or military strategy; rather, hers was the world of humdrum, everyday bureaucracy and, where it strayed beyond that, one of euphemisms and half-truths. It is a reminder that the eye of the storm is rarely the best place to provide a good view of events.

Consequently, if the reader is looking for a discussion of grand strategy or of how power was exercised in the Third Reich, they are going to find this book disappointing. But that larger picture was not the author's intention. The intention was to provide a lively narrative which drew on Schroeder's twelve years in close personal contact with one of the most notorious dictators in world history; to provide an insider's view, with pen portraits of Hitler's entourage and illuminating insights into the character of Hitler himself. In that ambition, one must admit, it succeeds admirably.

Roger Moorhouse, 2025

Note to the translated edition

In this translated edition we have added full names and dates in square brackets to help readers unfamiliar with some of the main people mentioned. There are also some extra translator's notes, indicated by *TN*.

EDITOR'S NOTE[1]

Albert Zoller is a reserve captain and comes from an old family from Metz.

In 1940 he shared the fate of many of his compatriots: the Gestapo expelled him and his family to the Free Zone. From there he went to Morocco. Assigned to a special service, he helped to organise the Allied troop landings in November 1942.

Then began for him the uninterrupted series of campaigns which were to take him from southern Tunisia to Berchtesgaden. Initially a liaison officer with the British 8th Army, he then joined the 7th American Army in Italy, with whom he landed at Saint-Tropez in August 1944. Captain Zoller specialised in interrogating prisoners and spent the entire campaign in France and Germany with the 7th Army Interrogation Center, where he quickly became a radar expert, interviewing German scientists and technicians, as well as many senior Wehrmacht officers.

When General Patch's army occupied Tyrol, it seized, in a huge sweep, almost all the high dignitaries of the Third Reich. The fallen leaders were gathered in an improvised camp in Augsburg and subjected to lengthy interrogations.

Captain Zoller thus had the opportunity to meet all those who, directly or indirectly, had lived in Hitler's wake. He recorded his discoveries and experiences in a manuscript entitled 'La Fortune changea de camp' [Fortune Changed Sides], which has only been partially published.

In this volume, Captain Zoller has delved into the dark mysteries of the Führer's personality. It reproduces with absolute fidelity the story of a secretary who spent twelve years alongside the latter and, for reasons that are easy to understand, the name of this woman must not be disclosed.

The book is written with complete objectivity. Some passages may be surprising, but we should not lose sight of the fact that the author intended to highlight all the still unknown facets of the daunting problem posed, for the historian, by this pathological subject: Hitler.

INTRODUCTION

April 1945: Germany is in agony. Under the furious assaults of the Allies, the area of the Third Reich is reduced to an ever-narrower strip of territory. It is an unprecedented example of a nation which, under the leadership of its leader, has allowed its last energies to be crushed and spends its final resources fighting the pressure from the two cylinders of a gigantic rolling mill: the invading armies.

Until the last minute, until the last cartridge, the fighting continued and the blood flowed. Flames of destruction rose to the sky until the last light of the twilight of a great country ... and a despicable regime!

It took the occupation of the capital to put an end to this titanic struggle, where the fallen colossus had continued to fight until the last convulsions of its ravaged body.

From this tumult and din emerged, enigmatically, the pale mask of Hitler. Who was this man who had been, for twelve years, the central figure of European history?

Volumes have been devoted to him, but they focus more on events where he was the driving force, or on the results of his actions and policies, rather than describing or examining the man himself. Satirists have taken up this pathological case, almost unique in history, less to explain it than to give free rein to a simple fantasy and to satisfy the curiosity of a gullible public.

The real actors in Hitler's drama, those who gravitated in his demonic orbit, are dead or ... silent. I had the opportunity to meet them at length in my capacity as an interrogation officer, attached to the 7th Army Interrogation Center of the United States Armed Forces.

One of Hitler's secretaries, whom I met in the Augsburg Camp in May 1945, where she was lost in a motley gathering of Wehrmacht, Party and government bigwigs, later brought her old master back to life before me, as she had observed him, as she had heard him speak.

I had a long discussion with Göring at the Augsburg Camp about the Hitler problem; with Funk, Schacht's successor; with Frick, the man who had given Hitler German citizenship; with von Warlimont, the head of the Führer's headquarters; with Dr Morell, his trusted physician; with Schaub, his adjutant, etc., etc.

In none of these men did I find a power of analysis comparable to that of this young girl, who was able to evoke Hitler with such perceptiveness, with such a gift of observation and precision of feelings that give her story a feeling of absolute sincerity.

Following the dissolution of the 7th Army Interrogation Center in December 1945, she was transferred to Nuremberg as a witness and I lost track of her. She was then sentenced to two years in an internment camp by a German denazification tribunal.

When she was released, a religious congregation took her in and employed her in heavy kitchen work. That is where I found her. By mutual agreement, we decided to write this book for the sole purpose of establishing the character and studying the psychology of Hitler, a neurotic of international crime.

Surprisingly, the leader of the Third Reich was in the habit of confiding in people, of delivering his intimate thoughts and visionary rants to his secretaries, with whom he took his meals and whose presence he required at the nocturnal teas with which he ended his working days, and at the breaking dawn of the next day.

In the pages that follow, the reader will discover an unknown Hitler. Behind the opaque curtain woven around him by propaganda and his prestige, you will see him live, act, struggle and collapse. You will find yourself in the presence of a man whose life, far from the crowds, unfolded in a double-sided and extraordinary atmosphere of stiff petty bourgeoisie and hallucinatory drama.

I cede the floor to the person who was, for many years, his closest collaborator. In terms of perfect objectivity, she presents the man whose tragic personality, to a superhuman degree, evokes the famous phrase: 'laugh or cry'.

A.Z.

I

The best ideas come to me at night.

Hitler

Hitler hated meeting people in his entourage who he was not used to seeing. This is why two of his secretaries – one of my colleagues and I – remained in his service for fifteen and twelve years respectively. Despite the disagreements and frictions that may have arisen, he did everything to keep us until the end.

Hitler was possessed by the demon of distrust. He never hired his private staff simply on recommendation. He only trusted them after having observed them at length and putting them to the test, by setting real traps for them.

As far as I am concerned, I must confess that I was surprised at the ease with which he took me into his service. Nothing in my past had particularly marked me out for such trust. My father, who had been a civil servant in Hanover, had always expressed violently democratic ideas. He died in 1926, when I was 17. I had already lost my mother a year earlier. Alone in the world and with no money, I became an office-worker and took shorthand typing courses.

At the beginning of 1930, I left a secretarial position in Munich and applied for a vacant typist position in the Party leadership.

Having come first out of eighty-seven competitors in the national shorthand competition, I was appointed secretary to Captain Pfeffer [Franz Pfeffer von Salomon (1888–1968)], who at that time was in charge of the SA. When Röhm [Ernst Röhm (1887–1934)] succeeded him in 1931, I was assigned to the economic department of the National Socialist movement.

I have always been very interested in fine arts and ethnography. I regularly attended evening classes organised by the Munich Teachers' College and gradually built up a personal library. This may have been the reason for my relationship with Hitler, on an intellectual and human level.

I must add, however, that I have a very developed critical instinct. I have always felt the need to get to the bottom of problems and to give my trust only with great caution. With that in mind, it is understandable that the twelve years I spent alongside Hitler were strewn with surprises and bitter disillusionment.

In 1933, it happened that Hitler's private secretary was away one day and he had an urgent memo to dictate, so I was asked to put myself at his disposal. When I entered his office, I was struck by his intense blue eyes, which scrutinised me profoundly, but kindly. His Austrian accent, his simplicity and the encouraging cordiality with which he received me pleasantly surprised me. He said a few words of welcome to me and, without further delay, got to the heart of the matter:

'I usually dictate directly to the machine. If you skip a word, it doesn't matter. This is just a draft.'

I told him that I was used to this kind of work and sat down at the typewriter. When he had finished, he thanked me warmly and gave me a box of sweets. Whenever I met him afterwards, he would greet me enthusiastically.

At the end of the year, I requested to be moved to Berlin due to problems I had experienced with the SS, following an anonymous denunciation. My wish was granted and I became secretary to Brückner [Wilhelm Brückner (1884–1954)], Hitler's adjutant, although the latter would sometimes ask me to help when he had long dictations to do. One day, his secretary was ill and I was put at his exclusive service. From then on, I was in Hitler's wake every day, except at weekends, when he still regularly went to Munich.

At that time, Hitler had a regular work schedule. At 11 o'clock he would cross through my office and spend the rest of the morning meeting with his colleagues. At 2 o'clock he passed by again, stopping to glance at the gifts that admirers had left every day: books, paintings, embroidery and other handicrafts. During these short moments, he would quickly dictate a few memos or sign urgent letters. In the afternoon, the meetings resumed and continued late into the evening.

He reserved his more important dictations until nighttime. His adjutant would come to tell me when he had decided to stay in the office: 'The Chief will dictate tonight. Be ready!'

This sentence triggered a real state of alert in the office. I dared not leave. I soon realised, however, that Hitler was not a model of punctuality when it came to this form of night work, and I would often wait for him eight or ten nights in a row, without him making a single appearance. This happened especially when he was preparing a speech for the Reichstag or the Party Congress. To my dismay, I had to come to terms with the fact that he had a habit of dictating these speeches right at the last moment, the day before he delivered them.

When the date of the speech had been published by the newspapers and I pointed out that it might be time to think about the dictation, I was answered evasively: 'The Chief is still waiting for a report from the embassy,' or, 'He wants to follow a diplomatic development whose solution could be decisive for his speech.'

It is obvious that, under such conditions, the work was carried out in an atmosphere of haste and panic. When the solemn moment finally came, Hitler asked us (he needed two secretaries for the larger dictations) to rest in the afternoon so that we were ready. He would spend those final moments thinking and jotting down some notes on a piece of paper. In these hours of meditation, no one was permitted to disturb him.

As soon as he had decided on the main points of his speech, an imperious ringing would call me. When I entered his office, I found him pacing nervously up and down. From time to time, he stopped in front of a portrait of Bismarck, which he looked at with wistful eyes, as if in prayer. He seemed to be begging the Iron Chancellor to give him the benefit of his experience in state affairs. With the mindless movement of a sleepwalker, he went from one piece of furniture to another, to correct the position of the miniatures that cluttered them. Then he would start walking quickly around the room, only to stop suddenly, as if paralysed. Still he would not look at me. Then he started dictating.

At first, the flow of his voice was normal, but as his thoughts developed, the cadence accelerated. The sentences followed one another without stopping, punctuated by the increasingly rapid steps with which he made his way around the room. Soon, the tempo became choppy and his voice swelled. Hitler dictated his speech with the same zealous passion he would use to deliver it to his audience the following day.

Hitler literally lived his speeches. When he wanted to give free rein to his emotions, he would stop pacing, his eyes staring at the ceiling at an imaginary spot from which he seemed to expect a special kind of grace. As soon as he spoke about Bolshevism, his voice would rise furiously and violent rushes of blood would redden his face. He then declaimed with such force that his voice could be heard in all the surrounding offices and, every time, the staff waiting nearby would ask me why the Chief had been in such a bad mood.

Once the dictation was over, Hitler regained his composure and even found a few kind words for his secretaries. A few hours later, he began the corrections. But again, he had to be reminded that the work was unfinished. Indeed, he would often not finish his manuscript until shortly before the scheduled time for his speech and would then spend the final moments rereading it and making corrections. When he had time, he liked to refine his vocabulary, seeking ever more subtle expressions and more striking formulas. He was convinced that it was difficult to read his corrections, each time asking me, 'Look carefully, my child, and see if you can decipher this annotation.'

When I read his corrections back to him without difficulty, he stared at me with that strange gaze over the rim of his glasses and admitted, with barely feigned resignation, 'I see you can read my writing even better than I can.'

His eyesight had noticeably deteriorated over the years, and because he wanted to avoid appearing in public wearing glasses at all costs, he had typewriters made with 12-mm high characters, thus allowing him to read his texts without difficulty.

When his speech hit the mark, Hitler gave the impression of having been relieved of a major problem. He had got into the habit of inviting the secretaries to his table and, during the meal, never failed to announce that he was satisfied with his writing and to predict that it would be a great success. He also invariably praised the professional abilities of his secretaries: 'They are so fast on their machines; they write faster than I can dictate. They really are typing queens', etc., etc.

Hitler often told me about the difficulties he had in finding young girls who would not lose their nerve when working with him: 'When I saw the blood rush to their heads as I started to speak, all I could do was send them on their way and try another one.'

For my part, I admit that working for him was not exactly easy. Even when he dictated normally, his pronunciation was not very accurate. The sound of his footsteps, the noise of the machine and the echo of his voice in the overly large office made some of his sentences completely incomprehensible. It took absolute concentration and considerable intuitive training to guess the ends of sentences and fill in the gaps. When Hitler was particularly angry, his feverish agitation would be passed on to his colleagues, and in such moments of crisis my strength was truly stretched to the limit.

Hitler was well aware he was wearing us out at this rate, but he did not want to hire other secretaries, saying he could not stand new faces around him. Consequently, my personal freedom was practically zero. I was at his disposal day and night and was not allowed to leave the headquarters without ensuring I could be reached by telephone, telegraph or even loudspeaker.

Hitler's principle of keeping a decision secret until the moment of its execution exerted a tyrannical pressure on everyone around him. Travel and journeys were always announced well in advance, but he reserved the right to make the departure time public only at the last minute. Throughout those days of fruitless waiting, we were extremely tense. During a conversation, if a reference was made to the influence he exercised over the freedom of his staff, he feigned astonishment, saying that he left everyone free to use their spare time as they saw fit. However, in truth, he never tolerated anyone having an independent private life.

During our long stays at the Berghof, he would gather his entire entourage in front of the fireplace in the great hall every evening. Like high school students, we were regularly deprived of 'going out'. It is true that these evenings by the fire were not without charm, when there were visitors, but it was often the same people who found themselves there day after day. It really did require strong control of one's nerves to sit through those endless meetings, in front of the unchanging decor of logs burning in the large fireplace. When someone was brave enough not to come to one of these sessions, Hitler would notice and express his displeasure.

In 1938 a new secretary was hired because of the frequent illnesses from which my friend suffered. The newcomer was remarkable not only for her professional abilities, but also for her beauty. From then on, two secretaries accompanied Hitler on all his trips. As he slept very badly, despite the sleeping pills, he made a habit of holding tea parties that lasted well into the night, which were attended by his secretaries, his aide-de-camp, his doctor and Bormann [Martin Bormann (1900–45)].

I spent a good part of my life on the special Führer train. During these trips, Hitler insisted the curtains of his saloon car be closed, even in the middle of summer. He wanted purely electric lighting because the sun annoyed him, although there was another reason for this, which was surprising to say the least: he liked the make-up of the new secretary I mentioned earlier so much that he wanted to emphasise it even more with artificial lighting. He would then pay her endless compliments, forcing the other men around him to do the same. Bormann, who was a bit dense, did so with a clumsiness that amused us all.

Conversation invariably revolved around his car journeys and it was only reasons of convenience that had prompted him to abandon the road. Hitler enjoyed these wild races across Germany, not only because he loved speed, but also because they gave him the opportunity to meet the population. A keen motorist, he designed various improvements which were successfully adopted by the Mercedes firm.

However, there were days when an exuberant kind of gaiety reigned on board the special train, when Hitler amused himself with his entourage by playing games. For example, we once counted the number of bearded men we met during the day, with a prize awarded to the person who saw the most. Other games of the same vintage put Hitler in an excellent mood, and in these moments of relaxation he began to mimic his former comrades in their gestures and way of speaking. He excelled in this kind of exercise and often made fun of foreign politicians whose facial expressions and failings he had observed during international conferences. He would perfectly imitate Victor Emmanuel's high-pitched laugh and amusingly demonstrate to us how, because of his short legs, the King of Italy's height remained the same whether he was sitting or standing.

In this pre-war period, Hitler still appreciated good spirits and humour. 'A joke, said at the right time, creates miracles in the most difficult situations,' he liked to say. 'I experienced it, not only during the 1914–18 war, but also during the period of struggle that preceded our seizure of power.' However, he changed completely as soon as the first setbacks hit Germany, becoming more withdrawn and hardly letting anyone approach him any more. The circle of friends he was accustomed to gathering every evening was shrinking every day until, finally, only his secretaries were allowed to share his solitary reveries. Until 1942, huge rooms and a certain decorum were needed to prepare an important diplomatic action or a grand operation, which the Berghof lent itself to admirably.

'It is in the majestic calm of the mountains that I have made my best decisions,' he said. 'Up there, I feel like I am hovering above earthly misery, above the unparalleled trials that strike my people, our worries and our difficulties. The unlimited view of the Salzburg plain allows me to escape from mundane problems and to hatch the brilliant ideas that turn the world upside down. In these moments, I no longer feel connected to mortals; my ideas go beyond human limits to translate into actions with infinite repercussions.'

By 1943, Hitler no longer felt the need for a grandiose framework to inspire new plans for his morbid fantasy. As his life became increasingly hermetic, he would crouch in his bunker with its bare, cold rooms, like a reptile that fears the broad light of day.

Indeed, this was how he conceived the Ardennes offensive, during a long illness in September 1944. For three weeks he lay in a bunker at his headquarters in East Prussia, the 'Wolfsschanze'.[1] In the heavy, humid atmosphere of that room, with no windows or natural light, just whitewashed concrete walls, his imagination operated far from the world of reality. The electric lights never went out. Only the automatic click of the oxygen machine renewing the stale air punctuated the course of his thoughts. The echoes of events outside did not reach him. His assistants filtered what information he received and in such an atmosphere, his fantasies developed like a poisonous plant in a hot house. He admitted no replies, no responses. On the smooth walls where nothing caught the eye, his imagination projected, in a stereotypical way, the world as he had built it, in his conviction of winning the war through this final battle. In a tomb-like atmosphere, this shell of a human, who lived only through the injections given to him by his doctor, Morell [Theodor Morell (1886–1948)], hatched plans for a new offensive without caring about the human sacrifices it would cost his people, who were already drained of blood.

When Hitler had decided on a strategic move, he would wait impatiently for the moment he deemed opportune to give the order to take action. However, his intuition played a decisive role in setting the date for the start of the offensive. Only the meteorologists, whom he consulted day after day, were still allowed to speak. The specialist who had predicted a period of fog for December 1944, which facilitated the concentration of troops before the start of the assault, later received a gold watch in thanks for his happy predictions.

'The secret of success lies in persistence,' he used to say.

Hitler's whole life was one of effort and struggle. Having long been the victor over the most formidable adversities, it was difficult for him to imagine that one day his star would meet such a lamentable end. When he spoke, whether to an individual or to a crowd, he fascinated them before imposing his will.

I have often wondered whether this was a phenomenon of pure hypnotism or just the manifestation of entirely external influences. It is true that Hitler knew how to attract the sympathy of those he was speaking to through innately simple manners and rare cordiality. Viennese blood flowed through his veins, which, further refined by artistic inclinations, gave him an indisputable charm.

It should be added that, even in his most extensive performances, he knew how to concentrate his ideas in concise and succinct formulas, which were declaimed in a tone of conviction such that it was easy for him to impress whomever he was speaking with favourably.

However, these outward manifestations of his personality are not enough to explain Hitler's hold over certain people. He gave off that magnetic energy that either brings people closer together or, on the contrary, pushes them apart. In his case, this magnetic radiation did not shine so much in its intensity, although it far exceeded that of the average man, but rather in its extent. The instrument of his magnetism was very large and acted in a surprising way in public meetings and before large crowds.

It was this extraordinary suggestive power which explains why men who came to see him in despair would afterwards leave full of confidence. His impact on his former comrades in arms had a very special intensity. For example, I remember that in March 1945, the Gauleiter from Danzig, Forster [Albert Forster (1902–52)], came to Berlin to request an audience with Hitler. I saw him as he arrived in my office, totally broken by events. He told me that he had had no choice but to confront the 1,100 Russian tanks massed in front of his city with nothing but four Tiger tanks, which did not even have enough fuel. Forster was determined not to mince his words and to expose Hitler to the whole grim reality of the circumstances.

Aware of the situation, I urged Forster to report the facts objectively and to bring the Führer to a decision. Forster replied: 'Don't worry! I won't hesitate to tell him everything, even if I risk being thrown out.'

What a surprise it was when he returned to my office after his meeting with Hitler. It was as if he had been transfigured: 'The Führer has promised me new divisions for Danzig!' Faced with my sceptical smile, he told me: 'It is true that I do not know where he could acquire them, but since he told me he would save Danzig, there is no reason to doubt it.'

I was really disappointed by Forster's words. This man who I had seen in my office a short time before, forcefully proclaiming that he was going to tell Hitler what he thought, had come back, convinced by empty words. It was Hitler's convincing power that had undoubtedly worked its magic on him.

I could cite countless examples where people of influence and rank were literally duped by Hitler. Afterwards, when they recognised that they had been grossly deceived, the fear of being accused of weakness made them carry out the orders they had been given regardless.

Hitler was aware of his power and increased his abilities through intense training. Better still, by adopting a simple and natural attitude, he knew that he was creating a better impression on the person he was speaking to once he had gained their trust.

One day, he complained of feeling fatigued after a Party Congress in Nuremberg. During a parade lasting for several hours, he had remained under a blazing sun, his arm raised in salute, trying, as he explained to me, to acknowledge each of the figures that had passed in front of him: 'Everyone must feel that I have singled them out personally, which is enormously tiring.' I learned later that a large number of men flattered themselves that they had been noticed by Hitler in that dense mass of columns.

We also knew about the enthusiasm his presence and speeches triggered in the crowds; for his followers it became a real obsession during each of his trips. While they had been a necessity for Hitler for a long time, these hysterical masses later became almost unbearable. People were simply massing in front of the hotel where we were staying, the movements of the crowd breaking against the building like the undertow of a stormy sea. These human waves endlessly chanted their desire to see their 'Führer' appear at the window. These demonstrations, repeated morning and evening, really tested our nerves. I wondered how Hitler could stand it. Yet I knew they acted on him like an indispensable tonic. For example, one morning, when his guards cleared the crowds, he became angry because he did not receive his usual applause when he left the hotel.

When Hitler was travelling the roads of Germany by car, his detachment had a lot to do to prevent accidents. It sometimes happened that some women, having seen him, remained on the spot as if paralysed and were then crushed by the cars following him. It was often necessary to push back the crowds because they stopped the traffic, with SS officers then having to stand on the running boards to prevent the fanatics from storming the car.

The same spectacles were repeated at train stations, when

people were crushed crossing the tracks as they rushed towards the Führer's special train. When he leaning out of the window, he shook hands with those who were besieging him, the doctor who accompanied him was always afraid that Hitler's arm would be torn off, while yet again, the SS struggled to contain this delirious enthusiasm.

As these demonstrations cost Hitler considerable time and often delayed his itinerary, his movements were subsequently kept secret, although the fear of attacks also justified such security measures.

Hitler was not only harsh and wilful with others but was equally so with himself. In the period before the war, he knew how to control his feelings admirably, exercising his domineering will over himself as well as over those around him. He did not tolerate fatigue and subjected his brain to constant work, forgetting that endless reading not only tired his eyesight, but that voluntary and constant insomnia was to the detriment of his intellectual capacities. He was possessed by the conviction that willpower alone was enough to achieve anything. It is no surprise that the trembling which affected his right hand really hurt his pride, and the realisation that he was not the master of a part of himself made him furious. When visitors stared at this hand in surprise, he would instinctively cover it with his other hand. Despite his best efforts, however, he was never able to control this tremor.

Nevertheless, although he gradually lost control of his nervous reactions, he remained the master of his feelings until the end. When, during a private conversation, he was given a message informing him of a disaster, he would keep his cool. Only the movement of his jaw betrayed his emotion as he continued the conversation with the same calm manner. An example of this would be when the RAF destroyed the Edertal dam [*TN*: likely the Edersee dam], leading to the flooding of a large part of the industrial Ruhr valley. Hitler's face turned to stone as he read the message, but that was all. No one would have known that such a cruel blow had just struck him. It was only after several hours, or sometimes even several days, that he would return to the event in question and give free rein to his impotent rage.

Hitler was also an astonishing master at keeping secrets. He was convinced that each of his associates should know only what was necessary for them to perform their duties. He never told us his secret intentions or informed us of the plans he was making and when in front of us would never have made the slightest allusion to the operations he was preparing.

The beginning of the campaign in the West was a striking example of this. On 10 May 1940 he informed his entourage that he was going to travel that very evening, with not a word said about the purpose and intentions of his journey. When asked how long the trip would take, he answered evasively that it might take a fortnight, perhaps a month, or even, if necessary, a year.

Everyone who was to accompany him were driven in the direction of Staaken, and we were all convinced we would be flying out of the airfield there. Yet to our surprise, Staaken was bypassed and we joined Hitler on his special train, which set off for northern Germany. The comments flew thick and fast, and when someone timidly asked if we were headed for Norway, he confirmed this hypothesis by asking 'if we had not forgotten our swimsuits'. The train continued in the same direction to Uelsen, where, in the middle of the night, it suddenly turned west. Instead of arriving in Norway, at dawn the next morning we instead found ourselves in Münster-Eifel, from where we headed to the Führer's war headquarters.

I know that Eva Braun herself was unaware of any of his plans. In the summer of 1941, when he was planning his campaign in the East, he apologised to her for having to go to Berlin for a few days but assured her that he would return immediately. In reality, he went to settle into his headquarters in East Prussia, from where he would direct the first assaults against Russia.

II

There is hardly a subject a man can think of, without another having already done so before him.

Hitler

By uttering this saying, Hitler himself acknowledged that he was not a creative spirit. His knowledge was only the fruit of labours of memory, accumulated over the years. Like a sponge dipped in water, his memory, which was simply prodigious, absorbed everything that could be of some use to him either through reading or conversation.

From a young age, Hitler's thirst for reading had been boundless. During his difficult adolescence in Vienna, he told me, he had read the 500 volumes that made up one of the municipal libraries. This passion for browsing and assimilating works dealing with the most diverse subjects allowed him to extend his knowledge to almost all areas of literature and science. It would always surprise me when he launched into a geographical description of a region or gave astonishingly precise presentations on the history of fine arts or discuss technical details of such high specialisations.

Everyone who had struggled alongside him at the beginning of his career as a popular orator were surprised by the extent of his knowledge. Even back then, he knew how to impose himself on those around him by using the remarkable abilities his memory gave him, which contributed greatly to his winning the total devotion of those rough men who made up his first team of followers. With extraordinary skill he was able to give them impassioned lectures on the history of Austria, factual lessons on the intrigues of the House of Habsburg and poignant descriptions of a dying Germany. On top of this, he could talk endlessly about the construction of churches, convents and castles, all with an absolutely astonishing wealth of detail.

Even in the years following his imprisonment in Landsberg, he diligently continued to study all the historical monuments erected in the various countries of Europe, often flattering himself that he knew their architectural details better than at least one expert in the country where the buildings were located.

The officers on his General Staff and the commanders of the major Wehrmacht units also admitted that his knowledge of the entire Wehrmacht's structure, even down to the smaller units, exceeded all imagination and that his knowledge of weaponry and military equipment was simply phenomenal. One day, his naval expert had a rather heated discussion with him over a technical detail relating to the steam turbines installed on board modern cruisers. The intransigence with which Hitler countered his argument irritated the expert so much that he lost his temper, and with a disdainful pout declared: 'How can you claim such a thing when you're not completely versed in such technical issues?' Hitler did not react brutally, as he would have done on other occasions, but instead invited the expert to sit down and proceeded to give him a presentation on the matter in such detail that even the professors at the Naval Academy would have been astonished.

During the endless daily discussions in which he took stock of the situation with his Wehrmacht advisers, he never ceased to amaze everyone. He was aware of events taking place on the vast expanses of the front, the history of a prominent unit, the numbers engaged in each operation and the continual movements of troops during an ever-changing war. Not only was he familiar with the composition of each army group down to division level, but not even the small, specialised units, such as heavy tank destroyer battalions, failed to escape his intelligence.

The mayor of Munich, with whom he liked to discuss plans for the reconstruction and beautification of the city, often told me of his surprise at seeing Hitler remember the most insignificant details they had discussed between themselves months before. He sometimes heard Hitler say to him in a tone of reproach: 'Did I not tell you six months ago that a certain detail was not to my taste?' and reproduce, almost word for word, the entire exchange of ideas that had taken place on that particular point.

When Hitler was in a good mood, he liked to give us detailed descriptions of the great receptions that had taken place at the Chancellery in the years before. His excellent visual memory allowed him to describe the outfits worn by the artists or distinguished guests who had attended, and he recounted the lighter as well as the more serious conversations he had had with one or other of the attendees. The same was true for his impressions of plays or films that were presented. With incredible detail, he brought to life the pieces he had seen as a young man, telling us the names of the actors as well as remembering what the critics had said. How could a human brain maintain so many facts and details?!

It is indisputable that from birth, Hitler was gifted with an uncommon memory, but his secret lay in the fact that he developed and refined it day after day. He explained to us that when he read, he tried to grasp the broad outlines of the subject and then immerse himself in it. I have already said that he had a kind of mania, during those nighttime teas, or when chatting by the fireside, of telling us what he had learned during his reading in order to anchor it in his brain. This sort of mental gymnastics had become almost a requirement for him, but he was convinced that most readers were ignorant and could not profit from such an exercise. Although he was rather messy in his work and hated going through and annotating files, Hitler had an admirably organised memory, a memory with so many layers and which he knew how to make the most of.

However, in his constant desire to outclass the person he was speaking to and surprise them with the extent of his knowledge, he was also very careful not to betray the sources of his knowledge. He knew how to make those who listened to him believe that his presentations were the fruits of his own reflections and critical wisdom. He could quote entire passages, giving the impression that such literature was all his own work and represented the depth of his personal knowledge. Almost everyone I spoke to on this subject was convinced that Hitler was a profound thinker, gifted with a singularly perceptive and refined analytical mind.

One day, I decided to get to the bottom of this, so when Hitler surprised us with a philosophical dissertation on one of his favourite subjects, I was surprised to discover that his entire tirade was nothing more than a regurgitation of a page from Schopenhauer [Arthur Schopenhauer (1788–1860)] that I had read not too long before. Gathering all my courage, I drew his attention to this curious coincidence. Somewhat surprised, Hitler flashed me one of his impenetrable gazes, before answering, in a pedagogic and protective tone: 'Remember, my child, that one man's knowledge almost always has its origins in another. Each man contributes only a tiny part to the whole of science.'

In that same convincing manner, Hitler would also speak of famous men, foreign countries, cities, buildings, theatrical performances, etc., etc., all without ever having known or visited them. The peremptory and sure way in which he expressed himself and the clear and distinct dialectic in which he formulated his thoughts would persuade his listeners that he had genuinely seen or experienced what he was talking about. You truly believed that he had thought or experienced everything he described in his long narratives with such astonishing wealth of precision. However, there, too, I once again quickly uncovered his stratagem when, one day, he gave us a harsh critique of a theatrical performance that I knew he had not attended. I told him how surprised I was to see him condemn directors and actors so uncompromisingly, especially knowing he had not seen the play. He started, as if bitten by a tarantula, and said to me: 'You're right, but … Miss Braun was there and shared her impressions with me.'

However, this prodigious gift the spirits had placed in his cradle diminished over time. I later noticed that, to his great despair, in the last years of the war his memory no longer allowed him to play the role of thinker and brilliant technician. In this area, as in many others, he had fallen back in line with the rest of us, and the weakening of this faculty made him lose one of the main facets of his prestige.

Even so, one should not believe that Hitler was interested in all subjects with the same degree of passion. Indeed, while art, technology and history were his favourite subjects, his education nevertheless contained considerable gaps. Thus, he had only very vague notions of the law and legislative questions, while economics and public finances overwhelmed him, and he had no understanding of administrative procedures. A wonderful organiser as long as it concerned the structure of his Party, he gave his Gauleiter and senior officials complete freedom to organise the country's major administrations. Unforgivable excesses were therefore allowed to be committed simply because Hitler was not interested in the problems involved.

It was this inertia and repugnance that partly explain the ascendancy Reichsleiter Bormann was able to have over him. A fierce organiser and a veritable Hercules of paperwork, Bormann chewed over Hitler's work and relieved him of all the boring issues. In return, he gradually became Germany's hidden master, keeping the Führer away from the events that ravaged the nation's morale.

Hitler considered Bormann to be the only one of his associates who knew how to put his conceptions and ideas into intelligent and clear formulas. Often, when we dared to warn him that public opinion described Bormann's administrative methods as inhumane, he answered us, in a tone that admitted no reply and with which he was accustomed to resolving such thorny and annoying questions, with these words, 'I know that Bormann is brutal, but everything I entrust to him, he carries out with remarkable punctuality; everything he does is stamped with common sense.'

Hitler knew that Bormann demanded complete dedication and total efficiency from his subordinates. When complaints from employees reached him, he would push them away with the explanation that Bormann himself worked like a beast of burden: 'It's thanks to his toughness and uncompromising methods that he's able to carry out the formidable programme with which I have charged him.'

Another time, he praised Bormann, explaining: 'His reports are so polished and detailed that all I have to do is put my signature to them. With Bormann, I can clear a pile of files in ten minutes, while with others, it might take me hours to make the same decisions. When I ask him to remind me in six months' time about this or that question, I'm sure he'll remember to do so on the exact date. He's the opposite of his brother, who forgets everything.'

The brother in question, Albert Bormann [1902–89], was part of Hitler's secretariat and was hated by his brother Martin for marrying a woman Martin did not like.

It was after Hess's [Rudolf Hess (1894–1987)] departure for

England that Bormann's dizzying rise began. Indeed, the very evening that Hess's famous escape became known, Bormann gave a grand reception at his villa in the Obersalzberg, as if he were celebrating a joyous event. Then, thanks to a little scheming, he succeeded in removing Wilhelm Brückner from the influential position he had held with the Führer since the heroic days of the Party's struggle for power. From then on, Bormann felt free to move forward and began to work feverishly, systematically having all the important positions on Hitler's General Staff filled by men of his own choosing. With Machiavellian skill, he was able to infiltrate all the departments, meaning there were few direct associates of Hitler who were not caught in Bormann's net of corruption and denunciation. Bormann had become the *éminence grise*; the man Hitler could no longer do without. It was thanks to him that Brückner's position was taken over by Schaub [Julius Schaub (1898–1967)], a man without class or character. The latter's nefarious role consisted of slipping into the Führer's complacent ears phrases that were skilfully measured out by the devious Bormann.

During the final years of the war, the Reichsleiter ruled Hitler's headquarters as the undisputed potentate. Almost all the staff had been replaced by creatures in his pay, all of whom he had pulled out of the ditch and hoisted to coveted positions. Needless to say, these profiteers were completely devoted to their benefactor and were quick to report the slightest gossip to him.

Once he was master of the place and had nothing more to fear from Hitler's entourage, Bormann hastened to remove any outside dangers that might have threatened him. He gradually built a veritable Chinese Great Wall around Hitler, which could only be breached if the person showed their credentials and revealed the purpose of their visit. With this, Bormann thus had absolute control over all the workings of the Reich.

As an example, I remember that in March 1945 Gauleiters Hofer [Franz Hofer (1902–75)] and Forster from the eastern regions had gone to Berlin to report to Hitler, without first referring to Bormann. When the latter's informants told him of this move, he immediately interrupted his stay at the Obersalzberg and rushed to Berlin to thwart the two Gauleiters, who were themselves alarmed by the imminent invasion of their territories by the Russian army. Bormann reprimanded them savagely for ignoring his instructions and advised them to return to their respective Gaus and to begin making defensive preparations there instead of coming to make trouble in Berlin.

Bormann had no friends; the only one I knew of was Hermann Fegelein [1906–45], Miss Braun's brother-in-law. A strong camaraderie seemed to bind these two men together, although this did not prevent Bormann having his best friend shot for secretly trying to flee Berlin a few days before the city fell.

Bormann was undoubtedly Hitler's evil genius. His thirst for power was insatiable. Not only had he succeeded in placing his master in complete physical and spiritual isolation by peppering his entire entourage with men at his mercy, but he also knew how to mix things up admirably whenever an opportunity arose for him to show off. I could cite countless examples where Bormann made a state affair of irrelevant incidents. There are thousands to choose from.

One day, the DNB[1] published a notice that declared a farmer had been sentenced to two months in prison for withholding a litre of milk each day for personal consumption. The photographer Hoffmann [Heinrich Hoffman (1885–1957)], to whom the incident was reported, also owned a farm and let slip the following remark: 'In that case, I'd deserve to go to prison for years because I bring five litres of milk back from my property every time I go there.'

This imprudent confession was faithfully reported by one of his informers to Bormann, who immediately took up his finest pen to write verbatim to the offender: 'The Führer has asked me to inform you that, according to the regulations in force, you are only entitled to half a litre of milk.'

Whenever a former companion of Hitler casually mentioned that he had noticed one or another influential member of the Party transgressing the regulations, Bormann immediately exploited the fact by sending a letter to the person concerned, which invariably began with these words: 'According to the statements of Herr So-and-so, the following anomalies have been noted in your administration …'

Here is a final example that characterises the methods Bormann used to distance Hitler from all those whose bluntness of speech and criticism he feared. One day, Hoffmann received a telephone call from Bormann, informing him that his intelligence service suspected Hoffmann of carrying paratyphoid bacilli and that he should henceforth refrain from seeing the Führer. Hoffmann, frightened by this communication, submitted himself to six months of medical observations by the greatest specialists in Vienna, but the results were negative. In March 1945 he returned to Berlin to justify himself following the slander of which he had been a victim. While he was enjoying a meal in the Chancellery, Bormann arrived at the table and shouted at him furiously: 'You're back! You should've stayed where you were. Instead of doing business with your photographs, you'd be better inventing rays that can knock enemy planes from the sky.'

Half an hour later, Hitler happened to pass through the same room. With a weary gesture, he signalled to his guests not to get up. Hoffmann, nevertheless, rose to greet the Führer. Hitler greeted him very coolly and asked, with a hint of a threat, if he was genuinely cured. Hoffmann's vehement protests and the production of the medical certificate attesting that he had never suffered from paratyphoid fever, failed to convince Hitler, who from then on avoided meeting his 'court photographer' and turned a deaf ear to all the arguments with which the latter tried to justify himself.

I later learned that Bormann had insinuated it was possible Hoffmann had sent his son, who had the same first name as his father, to Vienna, and that the medical certificate had been issued for Hoffmann Junior instead. Hitler was gullible enough to take this deceit seriously, and so the sinister pantomime that ravaged the nation's morale continued.

III

It is by speaking often about the same subject that we manage to grasp its main points and remember them.

Hitler

In his final years, Hitler led an increasingly irregular life. While for ordinary people, meals are set into an immutable order throughout the day, Hitler focused his life exclusively on his famous 'conferences', during which he discussed the situation with his associates. The duration of these sessions was essentially elastic, ranging from one to four hours and beyond, meaning meals were therefore delayed accordingly.

He usually had breakfast around 11.30, lunch between 2 and 5 o'clock, and dinner between 8 and midnight. After he had eaten, he would take an hour's rest and then call the second *Lagebesprechung* [briefing], which often lasted until dawn. After having settled his strategic concerns, Hitler would have tea around 4 or 5 o'clock in the morning. In the final years, his only company were the secretaries and sometimes Dr Morell or his adjutant, Schaub. In 1944, I sometimes found myself still sitting opposite Hitler and listening to him speak with feigned attention at 8 o'clock in the morning.

Hitler could talk endlessly. It was always he who provided the necessary impetus for the conversation, which often degenerated into an endless monologue in which he expounded his views on the most diverse subjects. Indeed, the most unexpected topics were discussed in these informal conversations, and it is true that he spoke on every theme with equal confidence and verve. Even today, I wonder why he sacrificed his night's rest like that, just to expound his theories to an audience who, very often, would have much preferred sleep to such monotonous chatter.

When he was preoccupied by a topic or question, he liked to discuss it endlessly. He told us that by talking about a problem, the words would always open up new horizons and allow him to understand the ins and outs that had previously escaped him.

'Speech', he told us, 'builds bridges to unknown horizons. The German language in particular, with its subtleties and precisions, allows us to explore new regions in the mind. This is why Germany has always been a land of blossoming thinkers and poets.'

It is impossible for me to recount everything Hitler told me during those nocturnal teas, over a period of about ten years, and I admit that fatigue often took over my attention and I would just nod along, completely absent-mindedly.

Hitler liked to recall childhood memories during these nocturnal conversations, especially when he was preoccupied, and his youthfulness easily emerged from the jumble of thoughts that were agitating him. 'I never loved my father,' he used to say, 'but I feared him all the same. He was very irascible and beat me for no reason. When he corrected me, my mother would tremble for me. One day, I read in an adventure novel that it was a sign of courage not to show any pain, so I resolved not to scream any more when my father beat me. A few days later, I had the opportunity to put my will to the test. My mother, frightened, ran to the door, as I silently counted the blows of the stick that lashed my bottom. When I triumphantly announced to her that I had received thirty-two strikes, she thought I had lost my mind. Oddly enough, from that day on I never had to repeat this experience; my father never touched me again.'

Later, Hitler said, after having come face-to-face with the harsh realities of life, he had felt the greatest respect for his father, who, an orphan raised in the countryside, had managed to embrace a career as a minor customs official. Thanks to his thrift and hard work, he had even been able to acquire a small farm. Hitler also liked to tell us about his mother's housekeeping skills, thanks to which the family property gradually grew larger.

However, he used to call his sisters 'turkeys'. He resented them, for example, for the lack of understanding they showed for his favourite pastime, which consisted of shooting with a rifle the rats that populated the small town's cemetery. He confessed to us that during his sister Angela's engagement, he had advised her fiancé, whom he liked a lot, to break everything off and not to bother with such a shambles.

At school, Hitler was the leader of a gang and was always ready to play pranks. He was stubborn and rebellious even as a child: one day a teacher absent-mindedly called him Hitter, so he refused to get up from his desk. The teacher looked him straight in the eye and, once again, said, 'Hitter', but the future Führer still refused to move. When the teacher finally lost patience, Hitler, still seated, answered him calmly: 'My name is Hitler. Not Hitter.'

During religious instruction, he used diabolical stratagems to annoy the good country priest, trying to prove to his fellow students that religion could not be taken seriously. One day, in front of the whole class, he claimed in all seriousness that God had not created mankind at all, but that he had read in a book that people were descended from monkeys. The next day he brought in a volume of Darwin as evidence, much to the shock of the religious studies teacher. His mother was summoned by the school principal, who threatened her with reprisals if she did not prevent her son from stuffing his head with such inappropriate reading material.

Hitler was interested in girls from a young age. He told us that during the evenings in Linz, when he saw a girl he was interested in, he would approach her directly. When a girl was accompanied by her mother, he asked if he was allowed to accompany them to their door and, if necessary, offered to help them to carry their bags.

At the office, too, he sought to attract the attention of young girls by performing various antics, such as brushing his non-existent moustache with his father's brush. These pranks caused the young girls to laugh wildly, and Hitler was happy with his little victories.

He also liked to tell us about his first attempts at smoking, when he had managed to smoke half a cigar before becoming terribly ill and being forced to run home. He told his mother that he had indigestion after eating cherries. The doctor, called in haste, searched through Hitler's pockets and found the cigar butt. 'Later,' Hitler added, 'I bought myself a long porcelain pipe and smoked like a chimney, even when lying down. One time I fell asleep and when I woke up the bedding was on fire. Afterwards, I resolved never to smoke again and have stuck to my vow.'

A similar incident occurred when, still a young man, Hitler had drunk some brandy. I had always felt it was difficult for him to explain why he had such a distaste for alcohol, and the fact that he never fully explained what had happened only piqued my curiosity. Finally, my insistence got the better of his reserve and he told me the following story:

'After passing our final exam, my classmates and I celebrated the event with a respectable number of litres at a country inn. It made me sick and I had to rush out into the yard several times. The next morning, I searched unsuccessfully for the school certificate my father had asked me for. My efforts having been in vain, I decided to ask my school principal for a copy. It was then that the latter made me wipe away the greatest shame of my youth by giving me the stained diploma; a farmer had fished it out of the manure heap and returned it to the school. I was so upset that I have never again swallowed a drop of alcohol in my life.'

During these nighttime talks, Hitler covered almost every area of human thought. However, I had a vague feeling that something was missing, and even today I find it hard to put my finger on what it was. In my opinion, there was a note of humanity missing in all that waffle, the great soul of a supposedly cultivated man. Hitler's library was devoid of classical authors and of any works imbued with humanism and spiritualism. He often openly regretted to me that he did not have time to read good literature, dealing instead with problems of the mind and being thus condemned to read nothing but technical works. This negative side of his development explains the many setbacks he consequently suffered on a psychological level.

Art took a very important place in his discourses. He considered ancient Greece and Rome to be the cradles of culture, where conceptions of the cosmos, of science and pure intellect had found their first expression. He often told me how pleased he was, during his trips to Rome and Florence, to have been able to admire those immortal masterpieces he had previously only seen as reproductions.

Hitler despised modern art, considering it too marked by Expressionist and Impressionist tendencies. This 'degenerate art' – an expression coined by him – was, in his opinion, the work of the Jews, who made a great deal of publicity around such senseless works in order to sell them at a high price, while they themselves took care to furnish their collections only with Old Masters. Few contemporary German painters found favour in the face of his fastidious criticism, although he often bought paintings he did not like in order to encourage various artists. 'Painters today', he said, 'will never have the attention to detail and patience that those of the great periods of art possessed.' Indeed, there were only two periods of art he approved of: Antiquity and Romanticism. He resented the Middle Ages and the Renaissance because he found them too tainted with Christianity.

He did everything he could to acquire ancient works. I once saw him happy as a child on the day when, through Mussolini, he managed to buy the famous *Discobolus* by Myron. However, I cannot say whether his overflowing enthusiasm was dictated by artistic exultation alone, or whether it was mixed with the vain satisfaction of possessing such a masterpiece.

It was in Linz, which he considered his hometown, where he wanted to build the most opulent art museum in Germany. The paintings were no longer to be hung on the walls in a random manner, but rather each work was to be highlighted in an appropriate setting. Each Master was to have a special room, furnished and decorated in the style of the period to which he belonged. As a result, all the great artistic currents of history would flourish in their own atmosphere.

Yet Hitler was not only bitten by the passion of collecting. As a teenager, his great ambition had been to enter the Academy of Fine Arts in Vienna. The drawing exam he had undergone had been satisfactory, but his admission was denied because his academic background was insufficient to follow the course of study. Every time Hitler recounted this painful disappointment, he became broody and angry. He would inevitably formulate his usual reproaches against the injustice of fate, whereby young people too often languish in obscurity because they come from poor parents. During this period, and also during the First World War, Hitler, not without talent, reproduced monuments and public buildings in watercolour with an almost photographic attention to detail.

Painting and drawing were to remain his life's 'hobby'. Even in his hectic life as the head of state, he still found time to exercise his talent. He always had a stack of glossy canvases within reach in his office, which he used in his moments of relaxation to reproduce whatever the moment inspired in him. He was very proud of these sketches and guarded them fiercely. If he wanted to please or reward me after an exhausting day of work, he would offer me one, but never without drawing my attention to the value of his gesture.

Hitler also had a real passion for architecture. He had read countless books on the subject and knew the characteristics of different periods right down to the smallest details. His knowledge in this matter was truly astonishing. He knew the dimensions and plans of all the important buildings in the world, and from an urban planning point of view, he believed Paris and Budapest dominated all other capital cities. During the war, he confided to me more than once that his greatest happiness would have been to take off his uniform and devote himself solely to all things art.

He had drawn up a titanic programme of reconstruction for the cities and monuments destroyed during the war. The new post-war plans for Berlin and Hamburg were simply colossal. Whenever during his speeches he said, 'I will make Berlin the most beautiful city in the world,' he would stand up straight with an attitude of indomitable pride.

During the most trying of times, the idea of rebuilding Germany filled him with unprecedented vigour. When he returned from exhausting meetings, drained, his eyes dark with fatigue, he would recover his vitality with astonishing rapidity if some expert offered to examine his new plans or models.

In March 1945, I again saw Hitler standing constantly in front of a wooden model of the city of Linz, showing how he planned to transform it. In those moments, he forgot about the war: he no longer felt tired and would spend hours explaining to us all the various details of the changes he had planned for his hometown.

Music, theatre and film interested him to a lesser degree. He preferred Richard Wagner, whom he considered the regenerative genius of German mysticism. To his ears, the musical language of the Bayreuth master sounded like divine poetry, and he had attended performances of some of Wagner's works up to 140 times. It was *Der Ring des Nibelungen* (*The Ring of the Nibelung*) and *Götterdämmerung* (*Twilight of the Gods*) that left the deepest impression on him. He supported Bayreuth financially and planned to make it easier for the German population to attend the festivals as part of a national pilgrimage, with the German Labour Front organising group trips for workers and employees. Hitler and his entourage made it their duty to spread enthusiasm for Wagner's work among all social classes. After Wagner, only Beethoven and Bruckner mattered to him, although some of Brahms's *Lieder* and passages from Hugo Wolff and Richard Strauss also found favour.

Hitler claimed to have a highly developed musical sense. When he whistled a song in front of Eva Braun and she pointed out that he was out of tune, he would adopt a dogmatic air in response, declaring, 'It's not me who's at fault; it's the composer who made a mistake.'

At one point he was entirely carried away by two operettas: *Die Fledermaus* and *The Merry Widow*. I remember a time when, night after night, he would play these records in front of the fire in the big fireplace. Even in the office, he would sometimes abandon all work to whistle these tunes as he stood in front of the window, his hands in his pockets, his gaze lost in the infinity of the sky. He was a sincere admirer of fashionable actors and star dancers, rewarding them with valuable gifts. During the war, he was happy to send them parcels of coffee and food and afterwards received their letters of thanks with pleasure.

During the hostilities, he had given up on hosting great artists at brilliant annual parties, and only saw the president of the Association of German Artists, the director von Ahrendt [*TN*: likely Benno von Arent (1898–1956)], who came to see us frequently at Hitler's headquarters and took part in the famous nighttime teas. Hitler would ask him about each of the artists he knew, and every time Ahrendt departed, Hitler would shake his hand emotionally and repeat in a resigned voice: 'It's fortunate that you come to join me in my solitude from time to time; for me you are the living link to a world of dreams to which I no longer have access.'

IV

I cannot afford to fall ill.

Hitler

These words characterise Hitler better than any extended quote. Like all men who believed themselves called to fulfil an historic mission, Hitler was anxious that he would not have enough time to complete his work. This is why, under his personal leadership, all major projects were conceived and executed with a fury and haste that was far from in keeping with the methodical German spirit. The four-year plan, rearmament, the conduct of various campaigns, all were pushed forward with such haste and panic that the outside world no longer understood what was going on. The German population, which was accustomed to thoughtful and orderly work, was astounded by the feverish and agitated pace with which events and projects collided under the tireless direction of Hitler himself. How many times did I hear the following exclamation from leaders of German industry and politics: 'Germany has become a veritable madhouse. We are transforming and rebuilding with such haste that order is left to suffer. Everything is upside down. Let's hope it doesn't all lead to disaster!'

Hitler, who demanded the maximum performance from

his subordinates, was hard on himself and worked to the point of exhaustion. This is why the question of his health and the astonishing story of his personal doctors took on such importance. One may wonder whether this man's insane ideology, his uncontrolled reactions, which arose under the influence of an irrational impulse, were further reinforced by the hothouse atmosphere in which he delighted; or whether, on the contrary, his degenerate nature needed such an atmosphere to give birth to his extravagant thoughts and conceptions.

It is a fact that towards the end of his life, Hitler was nothing more than a physical and mental wreck. The collapse of his physical strength and the degeneration of his mind occurred in parallel.

In the first years after seizing power, he did not need a specialist doctor, and the only person responsible for his health was Dr Karl Brandt [1904–48], whom Hitler considered a friend. Over the years, Brandt called upon two other top-class surgeons, Dr von Hasselbach [Hanskarl von Hasselbach (1903–81)] and Professor Werner Haase [1900–50], who shared the formidable task of looking after Hitler's physical well-being. Hitler had always suffered from stomach and intestinal ailments. However, little by little, his illnesses developed to such an extent that he had to submit to an extremely rigorous diet. He had already been a vegetarian since 1931, which considerably reduced the number of dishes his cook was able to prepare.

On the advice of his photographer Hoffmann, Hitler agreed to meet with Dr Morell, who after his first examination, diagnosed a disease of the inner wall of the intestines. Morell set about reconstructing Hitler's intestinal flora and, for a year and a half, Hitler regularly took a Morell specialty called 'Mutoflora'. I do not know if this product helped to heal his intestines, but it is true that the eczema Hitler had suffered from for a long time on his leg was healed very quickly, and this unexpected result soon meant Dr Morell earned the Führer's confidence. Always in a hurry to get the most out of his working day, even the symptoms of a simple cold would cause him to suffer from an anxious depression. He hated staying in bed, which explains the great success of Morell's methods, which frequently succeeded in stopping a disease in its tracks through special injections.

The intrigues being woven around the patient and the struggles waged by those who were responsible for caring for him cast an unpleasant light on the entourage that Hitler had chosen for himself. Professors and academics showed a barely veiled contempt for Morell, whose unsettling personality was anything but formal. He was constantly the target of harsh criticism for his overly keen business sense, his endless worrying about being forgotten about when it came to receiving any medals, his appearance of a rough-hewn oriental, the questionable cleanliness of his medical instruments and, above all, because of the mysterious and generally considered harmful medicines he administered to the Führer.

Hitler, however, was not swayed by these attacks: 'These idiots (meaning Brandt, von Hasselbach, etc.) were unable to relieve me or find me a real specialist in internal diseases. They're only good at calling Morell a charlatan. But Morell cured me. My eczema is gone and I can eat normally again. They forget that I don't have time to be in bed with the flu. I've not had a proper day's holiday since 1920. I'm aware of everything that's going on and know everything that's happening. When I stay in my beloved mountains, the work continues in Berlin according to my instructions, as if I were there. I don't have time to be sick. These gentlemen need to understand that once and for all.'

However, the relentless work and the worries caused by the setbacks of the war undermined Hitler's health, and from winter 1941–2, Morell watched over him day and night, giving him intravenous and intramuscular injections every three days. In the end, these mysterious injections were being given to him almost every day. Morell explained to me that the serum in question contained grape juice, vitamins A, B, C, E, and hormones. In the latter years, when Hitler flew into a violent rage, his episodes were followed by painful stomach spasms. Whenever this happened, Morell would rush to apply a secret remedy only he knew the ingredients of, which had the gift of restoring a soothing calm to the patient – a remedy Hitler considered to be absolutely miraculous.

Hitler's decline began to worsen rapidly from the beginning of 1944. His left hand and right leg would shake with a constant nervous tremor, and it even seemed as if the leg was slightly paralysed because he would drag it a little. His valet was quick to ensure Hitler had a special cushion whenever he lay down. I could see in Hitler's eyes a furious desire to stop him from doing this, but it seems the relief it offered was such that he preferred such mortification of his pride to the throbbing pain.

After the assassination attempt of 20 July 1944, Dr Gising [*TN*: likely Erwin Giesing], who was treating Hitler's ears, discovered some 'anti-gas' tablets on his table one day. When he asked him how many he was taking, Hitler answered: 'Up to seventeen a day.' Dr Gising was appalled that Dr Morell would allow Hitler to consume such quantities. The doctors were alerted and, after a council of war, decided to warn the Führer officially of the disastrous effect such pills had on his body. They claimed that the trembling of his hand and leg, as well as the increasing weakening of his eyesight, were largely due to this drug. In the meantime, Reichsleiter Bormann had had the pills in question analysed and obtained a certificate stating they were absolutely harmless, and that it was therefore possible for a man to take them in such quantities. Bormann had no trouble convincing Hitler of Morell's good faith, and the incident led to the immediate dismissal of Drs Brandt and von Hasselbach.

Yet this does not mean that Hitler had absolute confidence in Morell. On the contrary, his distrust of him grew day by day. Every drug Morell proposed was carefully studied by Hitler, who read the instructions and what it would do for him with great attention. If, unfortunately, the shape of the drug container changed even in the slightest, Hitler would demand an explanation, wanting to know the reason for the change right down to the smallest details. Here again, his memory served him well, and it was therefore easy for him to recollect everything relating to each medicine. He had taken to involving Morell in lengthy discussions about the curative effects of the proposed remedies, and systematically tried to call Morell's assurances into question. As the doctor's memory weakened, it was difficult for him to sustain these indirect interrogations and to answer the punctilious questions put to him with the necessary precision required. Whenever he got the slightest detail wrong, Hitler growled, and his distrust took over once again.

Hitler suffered terribly from this continual haunted existence and confided to me that he had tried in vain to escape from it. Indeed, it is difficult to find other examples in history of statesmen who lived in such a psychosis of mistrust and fear. This near-madness of persecution was certainly not calculated to leave Hitler with the clarity of mind and judgement that would have allowed him to avoid the fatal errors committed with blind obstinacy during the final years of his reign.

His fear of falling victim to a contagious disease was at least as strong as his dread of a possible attack. As soon as one of his colleagues suffered from a slight cold, they were strictly forbidden to go near him. Hitler justified these measures with the constantly repeated assertion that, 'I have neither the time nor the right to be sick.' Despite these strict instructions, if a sick person had ventured into his vicinity, he immediately took preventive measures against possible contamination, even going so far as to sprinkle his tea with a few drops of alcohol. His doctors often told me what a difficult patient he was; his need to know and understand everything required hours of explanations for merely the slightest intervention. He would always consult a thick medical dictionary, and if he ever doubted the curative effects of a particular medicine, he would violently refuse to take it. The most scientific and sensible explanations had no effect on him. Such controversies invariably ended with an explosion of anger from the Führer, but not with the same hysterical violence as those he had with his generals.

Hitler had a real aversion to undressing in front of anyone. Until November 1944, he had refused Dr Morell's advice, under the most varied pretexts, to do so, but when the doctor took the liberty of reminding him that he had promised to let himself be X-rayed, Hitler lost all control and the shrill bursts of his voice echoed all the way down to the antechamber where I stood.

Hitler hardly varied his repertoire in his fits of indignation towards his doctors: 'What's got into you, giving me orders! I'm in charge here and no one else. People seem to have forgotten this too easily recently. If you dare to do this again, I'll fire you immediately. I'm old enough to know what I need to do for my own health.'

One day, Morell dared to ask him the real reason why he refused to take a particular treatment, and Hitler answered him coldly, 'It's because I don't want it. That's all.' With untiring zeal, Morell continued to offer him different medicines until one day, in despair after Hitler's latest refusal, he cried out, 'But, my Führer, have I not taken responsibility for looking after your health? If anything ever happened to you!!!'

Hitler pierced him with that mysterious gaze in which flickered a wicked flame. Then, emphasising each word, detaching each syllable in cruel delight, he fired this sentence at him: 'Morell, if anything ever happened to me, your life would be worthless too.' As he said this, he made a gesture with his hand in which he seemed to crush a handful of air.

Is it any wonder that Hitler's health and his relationship with his doctors had the most dramatic repercussions on everyone around him? I cannot cite a specific example, but it is certain that more than one decision or interview with a foreign diplomat was influenced by the physical disposition in which Hitler found himself.

The question of the Führer's health had become a genuine national issue. I know that Himmler [Heinrich Himmler (1900–45)], the mysterious mastermind behind all events in the Third Reich, also wanted to maintain control over it. Morell was therefore constantly exposed to underhand manoeuvres from him. When Professor Brandt and Dr von Hasselbach lost Hitler's confidence, a young SS doctor called Dr Sturmfeger [*TN*: likely Ludwig Stumpfegger (1910–45)] took their place and it was thanks to him that nothing escaped the leader of the black militia. Himmler's 'eye' was mainly responsible for monitoring Morell's actions, and it was not long before the doctor became aware of this and from then on lived in permanent terror. When Himmler summoned him unexpectedly to his headquarters at the beginning of 1944, before undertaking the journey Morell confided to me that he was tormented by fear. However, he was very surprised to find that Himmler had not asked him to account for his special treatments. Instead, very kindly, Himmler asked him to do him the service of influencing Hitler to accept the care of his personal masseur, who had a great professional reputation. Morell refused to comply with this request, knowing in advance that Hitler would never agree to be massaged by this newcomer. This was not only out of instinctive distrust, but above all because of his repulsion of showing himself in an undressed state. Only in his last few months did Hitler resort to the care of this masseur, the scheming Himmler having finally succeeded in his enterprise.

Morell was well aware that he was nothing more than a pawn in Himmler's infernal game. His mortal anxiety was constantly balanced between the increasingly disagreeable character of the patient he was treating and the relentless surveillance he was kept under by the Third Reich's Chief of Police.

*

Hitler was obsessed with the idea of reaching a very old age, often retuning to the issue in his conversations. He was convinced that science would one day succeed in pushing back the fateful limits of human life. Laboratory experiments had yielded encouraging results, while Morell had led Hitler to believe that elephants reached a ripe old age because they ate a certain grass grown in India. If circumstance had permitted it, I am convinced that Hitler would have sent an expedition to India to carry out research.

Thanks to his exclusively vegetarian diet and his renunciation of tobacco and alcohol, Hitler expected to add a few years on to his lifespan to complete the work of his earthly mission. And yet, he never realised that the artificial and unnatural life he was actually living would inevitably lead him to premature physical decline. This abnormal side of his existence, his frantic work at night that only allowed him brief moments of sleep thanks to the increasing number of sleeping pills he took, made him a human wreck at an age when normal men are at the peak of their strength.

I should add that Hitler did not play any sport. Horses frightened him, he hated snow, and bright sunshine hurt him. He also had a great fear of water. He never agreed to go canoeing. I do not think he even knew how to swim. He told me one day, 'The movement man makes in the accomplishment of his daily work gives him enough exercise to keep his body in shape.' Having said that, this did not prevent him from greatly admiring German athletes.

Hitler was unconsciously ruining his health, which deteriorated noticeably from 1942. The nervous trembling in his hand troubled him more and more, and his furious outbursts were immediately followed by nervous depression and stomach cramps that shook him with pain. In those moments of crisis, Morell was always there with his syringe to ease his suffering. At the end of 1944, Hitler developed jaundice after a stormy argument with Göring [Hermann Göring (1893–1946)]. Once again, Morell and his syringe worked to calm and reinvigorate this drug-filled rag.

V

I will never kiss a woman who smokes.

Hitler

Hitler literally lived like a Spartan, eating only vegetarian meals and abstaining from coffee, black tea and alcohol. He was so convinced of the harmful powers of meat, alcohol and nicotine that he returned to the subject constantly during conversations, seeking to make us share his aversion. Eating meat, he claimed, created the need for alcohol. Consuming alcohol, meanwhile, encouraged smoking, and thus one vice led to another, plunging an entire population into terrible misery. In his opinion, nicotine was even more dangerous than alcohol and he considered it a terrible poison, whose dire consequences only became apparent years later. Smoking dulls the mind and narrows the arteries, while a general weakening of the constitution is common among all heavy smokers. Indeed, Hitler once joked that: 'A really good way to get rid of your enemies is to offer them cigarettes.'

Whenever anyone dared to contradict him on these points, Hitler would see red and the unfortunate man would immediately lose all esteem in his eyes. How many times did he say to me with great seriousness: 'If I ever found out that Eva was secretly smoking, I would end our affair immediately.' Hitler even toyed with the idea of banning tobacco and cigarettes after the war and was convinced that he would thus render the greatest service to his people.

He had no real notion of money and property, which were merely vague concepts for him. His only luxuries were concentrated in large rooms he decorated with tapestries, old paintings, valuable ornaments and flowers. On a personal level, he was incredibly lax and negligent. His wardrobe was sparse and devoid of any refinement; fashion did not exist for him. All he asked was that his shoes did not squeeze his feet and that his suits did not hinder his movements. As it was his habit when speaking to emphasise his sentences with broad, violent gestures, the sleeves of his jackets were consequently cut very wide. He hated having fitting sessions at the tailors', and always had three or four suits made at a time to avoid going, all of which were then cut in the same way and often in the same fabric. He was uninterested in ties, so when he saw one that he liked, he immediately bought half a dozen of the same design.

During the war, he wore a ready-made tie with his uniform, which he fixed with an automatic action and thus avoided wasting precious time tying the knot. While he was always seen wrapped in a putty-coloured trench coat with a grey velvet hat when he first came to power, in the final years, when he was at the Obersalzberg, he wore a shapeless, dirty grey, long jacket and a grey cap with an oversized black visor. The visor hid almost the entire upper part of his face and was a constant source of astonishment among his guests, but he ignored all the friendly criticism that was levelled at him, arguing that it protected his eyes from the sun, which he hated.

Whenever guests or those who were close to him suggested he dress a little more elegantly, he would scowl and make his displeasure very clear. Only clothes he felt comfortable in mattered to him and he detested dressing up for official ceremonies. He could not understand why one had to squeeze into a rigid shell just to receive foreign diplomats. Tired of the war, even the tuxedo was no match for his practicality, and he had a two-button one made for himself, which was then eagerly imitated by many in his entourage.

He never wore jewellery or a wristwatch and until the end, only his big gold watch, which almost never worked, lay chainless in one of his jacket pockets. He regularly forgot to wind it up and so was frequently asking his employees or guests for the time, but always with good humour and irony: 'Once again my "regulator" has stopped.'

It is true that, in his eyes, a watch did not have the same role as it did for ordinary mortals. It was his valet who took on the role instead, waking him up in the morning and reminding him of essential meetings during the day.

Hitler always slept behind a locked and bolted door, and his valet would knock at the appointed time (usually around 11 o'clock), shouting: 'Good morning, my Führer! It's time to get up.' At the same time, he would leave the morning newspapers and reports outside the door, which Hitler would then pick up and read through quickly – his valet never saw him undress or in his nightshirt.

Around noon, Hitler would ring the bell for breakfast, which in the early years still consisted of a glass of milk and some bread. Later, he ate only a grated apple, and, towards the end, a kind of compote prepared according to a Swiss doctor's recipe, which consisted of milk, oatmeal, grated apples, nuts, lemon and a number of other products. While he was eating his breakfast, his adjutant would bring him urgent messages and report on the events of the night, before setting out his schedule for the day. When he stayed at the Berghof, Hitler would gather his staff in the great hall for the morning report and felt a physical need to be in that room of such gigantic dimensions. He would walk back and forth, chatting with everyone, and from time to time his gaze would rest on the snow-capped peaks of the Alps, the panoramic view of which was framed in an immense shop-sized window.

During these meetings, Hitler would often forget about lunch, and so his guests had to wait patiently out on the large terrace or in their rooms. When he finally arrived, he greeted Eva Braun first, then each of the guests, apologising for his delay. In the early years, he only kissed the hands of married women, but later got into the habit of doing this with younger girls as well. Hitler then greeted the male guests and chatted with them very enthusiastically until the head waiter entered and announced, 'My Führer, lunch is served. Please lead Frau or Fräulein So-and-so to the table.' Hitler would then go to find his table companion, offer her his arm, and lead her to the dining room. Eva Braun would follow on the arm of her own table companion, followed by the other couples.

At the table, Hitler always took the middle seat, facing the windows. Eva Braun invariably sat to his left. The length of the meal depended on the afternoon's programme. The atmosphere at the table was never the same and had its ups and downs depending on the events of the day. Hitler's mood was reflected in everything he did. One day these meals would be bathed in an icy indifference and the next would be almost exuberantly lively. It all depended on the mood of the master of the house at the time.

Hitler was very frugal. He liked single dishes and had a particular weakness for green beans, followed by peas and lentils. There was no difference between the meal served to him and that of the guests, the only distinction being that his had never been in contact with any meat or fat. He literally hated meat and even refused to eat any sort of meaty broth. He was convinced the consumption of meat prevented man from leading a natural life. When we discussed this point, he cited horses and elephants as examples of animals endowed with great strength, while dogs, which are essentially carnivores, quickly become out of breath from exertion.

To dissuade his guests from eating meat, he liked to discuss at the table what the dead and rotten meat represented; whenever a lady gave him a pleading look to stop these graphic descriptions, it only encouraged him to exaggerate further. He regarded the fact that people's appetites were spoiled following these conversations about the origin of meat as a confirmation of his principles. Despite this, he never practised this bizarre proselytising in front of foreign guests.

When someone praised his vegetarian diet, however, he would launch into euphoric descriptions of how the ingredients were produced. He would mimic the farmer sowing his field with broad, majestic gestures. Then when the wheat took root, how it would grow and become a sea of green, which then gradually turned golden in the sun. In his eyes, these bucolic images argued for a return to the land and the natural products it provides for human nourishment. But these poetic tirades always ended on his favourite theme: the disgust that the consumption of meat must inspire in every man. He had a way of describing the bloody work in the slaughterhouses, the butchering of the animals and the cutting up of the carcasses that made even the hungriest diners feel nauseous. To make up for this, he would finish by declaring that he had had no intention of forcing anyone to eat like him, as it might result in no one accepting his invitations any more.

After lunch, Hitler usually called his guests together for a meeting, and the group would take a walk to the small summer house, located about half an hour's walk from the Berghof. Hitler would walk in front with the guest of honour, while the others followed at such a distance that their conversation could not be heard. The whole company would then gather on the pavilion's small plateau and admire the majestic panorama of the Alps, before retiring to take tea.

If the conversation flagged, Hitler would try to liven it up by expanding on his nebulous theories about racism, or by recalling the happy times of his struggle for power. However, he was often seized with sudden fatigue after having taken his chocolate and his piece of apple pie. We would then see him curl up in the back of his chair and place his hand in front of his eyes as he simply fell asleep.

Eva Braun would then begin to chatter loudly, knowing from experience that a respectful silence would have disturbed her master's sleep. When it was time to leave, she would wake Hitler discreetly. The return to the Berghof was always by car.

Hitler rarely visited the famous 'teahouse', located 2,000 metres above sea level on a steep rock overlooking the whole of Berchtesgaden. This 'Eagle's Nest' was the brainchild of Bormann, with the building of the road and the drilling of the tunnel leading to the curious construction costing enormous amounts of money. A whole army of workers had been mobilised. Hitler was very proud of his Eagle's Nest, but the elevator ride to the top made his heart pound and he only went there when foreign statesmen came, although he was always dazzled by the magical sight of the rocky escarpments rising from the clouds.

I have already said that Hitler was a night owl, and as evening fell, his whole personality would take on a more open and animated character. Dinners at the Berghof therefore had a completely different feel to lunches.

Hitler liked women who adorned themselves with natural flowers. He would sometimes even take flowers used to decorate the table and throw them, with an engaging air, towards his guests. When the women he had shown an interest in had pinned them in their hair or on their dress, Hitler always paid them a charming compliment. When a woman came to the table wearing flowers whose colour he did not like, he would quickly choose others from a vase and hand them to her, remarking that they suited the paleness of her complexion or the colour of her dress much better. He rarely talked about fashion but knew how to accessorise an outfit and to compliment the person wearing it with excellent taste. On the other hand, he openly expressed his aversion to certain novelties, such as shoes with cork soles.

However, I am convinced that this was all just a ruse. On several occasions I heard Hitler express his admiration to Eva Braun for the 'new' dress she was wearing, only for her to respond briskly that she had already worn it more than once.

After dinner, the guests would gather in a small living room, which was particularly popular with women because it was heated by a huge, tiled stove. I should explain that Hitler, who hated the sun, bought the Berghof because it was on the northern slope of the Obersalzberg. The house was consequently in the shade almost all day long, and the thick walls prevented the heat of the day from penetrating the building. This meant it was cool there in the middle of summer but was freezing when it rained. Hitler liked the cold, but his guests found it very uncomfortable and rushed to the bench that ran around the tiled stove as soon as they could.

In one corner of the room was a complete collection of encyclopedias, and if, in the course of a conversation, the opinions of the guests differed on details such as the width of a river or the population of a town, etc., these were used to decide the question. With the meticulous accuracy he displayed in all things, Hitler would consult two different editions to be sure his facts were straight. It was in this small living room that he would speak privately with one guest or another, but when he was finished, he would ask everyone to follow him into the great hall to take a seat in front of the famous fireplace. To the great displeasure of those who were chilly, like me, the fire was not always lit, because only Hitler could order this to be done.

Eva Braun would sit on the right of the Führer, who would then designate the person to whom he would reserve the honour of sitting on his left. Hitler almost always led the conversation, sharing his impressions of any foreign diplomats he had met during the day before giving extensive explanations about the country in question. He was morbidly curious, however, and would continue to observe everyone as he spoke. If a group of guests whispered in a corner or someone started laughing unexpectedly, he immediately wanted to know the reasons why. In the pre-war period, we often used such a ploy to communicate things that otherwise would have been impossible to speak to him about. When he saw two heads coming together and whispering, he demanded to know what was going on and we would tell him news that, officially, it would not have been advisable to mention.

These sessions in front of the fireplace would end around 3 o'clock in the morning, with Eva Braun always retiring before him.

Sundays brought no festivities to the daily schedule. Hitler hated Easter, Christmas, etc. Ever since the death of his niece, Geli Raubal [1908–31], Christmas had become a real martyrdom for him. He allowed a Christmas tree to be positioned in a corner of the hall, but forbade the singing of carols and in later years even banned the lighting of the tree candles. I know of nothing sadder and more depressing than a Christmas spent with Hitler!

New Year, on the other hand, was celebrated according to tradition, with sumptuous meals and champagne. At the stroke of midnight, Hitler dipped his lips into a glass of sparkling wine and toasted the New Year with his guests, each time making a horrified face as if he had swallowed poison. It was incomprehensible to him that people could like this 'vinegar water'. Only once did I see him enjoy a glass of vintage wine, which he had been given for Christmas 1944, although when they tried to pour him another glass, he pushed it away sharply. He tried some again the next day, but his aversion to alcohol had taken over.

On New Year's Eve, Hitler went with his guests to the terrace of his villa to greet the inhabitants of Berchtesgaden, who were firing mortar salvos, before signing the menu for each of his guests and having a group photograph taken.

His birthdays were nothing special. When his immediate entourage passed on their best wishes, he would toast along with the rest of us, but each time making that same disgusted grimace at the champagne. Then in the afternoon, he would gather together all the children of Obersalzberg and stuff them with cocoa and cakes.

His only entertainment was receiving the president of the Munich Magicians' Club. Hitler followed his exhibitions and tricks with great interest and did not hesitate to compliment him. I never heard him laugh out loud, though. When a performance was amusing and he found himself sharing in the general joy, the most he would utter was a small, high-pitched chuckle, just as he did when reading some book and rejoiced at the misadventures of a naughty boy. He did not know how to express his joy with a straightforward laugh, and I only saw him lose his composure on two occasions.

The first was in the spring of 1939. Recent events had put the nerves of Hitler's entourage to a severe test. After the Führer had been conferring with Hácha [Emil Hácha (1872–1945)], the president of the Czech Republic, for three hours, we all knew how high the stakes were, and that peace or war could depend on the outcome. In our office, my senior colleague and I waited anxiously as the endless hours passed by.

Suddenly the door opened, pushed by two giant SS men. Hitler rushed towards us; his expression transfigured. 'My children!' he cried. 'Quickly, a kiss on both my cheeks. Quickly!' Stunned by such extravagance, we complied. Immediately afterwards, Hitler exclaimed, 'My children. I have good news to tell you. Hácha has just signed. This is the greatest triumph of my life! I will go down in history as the greatest German ever.'

The second time was in the Eifel, in June 1940, when Hitler was told that France had requested an armistice. He was literally shaking with a frenzied exuberance, and so the Master of the Great Reich began performing an uncoordinated, jerking dance, all under the watchful gaze of his astonished generals.

VI

The prettiest women are rightly given to the fighters.

Hitler

Why did Hitler never marry? It is a question we asked him often, but his answers gave no indication of the deeper reasons why he had taken a vow of celibacy; a vow he only broke on the eve of his suicide.

He limited himself to explaining in somewhat dry sentences that his marriage would cause his intellectual forces to dissipate. He added that a statesman could only sacrifice himself entirely for the happiness of his people on the condition that he gave them his whole being and pursued the proposed goal with an exclusive rigour. He cited examples of statesmen whose preoccupations, aroused by family matters, had made them forget their obligations to their people. 'The strongest characters', he said, 'have collapsed because of this and we have seen men, fiercely determined to succeed in the path they had chosen, instead fall into indecision and inaction.' He concluded by declaring that the importance of his mission forbade him from taking such risks.

This was all said with such seriousness and in such an authoritative tone that Hitler managed to satisfy our curiosity and convince even the most sceptical among us, and so the question abated. But the real reasons why he married merely hours before he passed into nothingness constitute one of the most tragically cruel aspects of his life.

He had loved Geli Raubal, the daughter of his half-sister Angela, with such passion that it was impossible for him to think of marrying another woman after his niece's tragic death. He often confessed to me that she had fulfilled the most absolute ideal he had ever had of a woman, and that it was she he would have married one day, if tragic circumstances had not taken her from him.

Geli was 16 or 17 years old when her uncle brought her from Vienna. She was a tall, dark-haired girl with hazel eyes and a melodious voice. At first Hitler treated her like a big child; he made her take singing lessons and jealously watched over relationships she shared with others.

In 1927, when Geli became secretly engaged to Emil Maurice, Hitler's chauffeur, her uncle, in a fit of fury, ordered the man to break off the planned union, while also threatening him with immediate dismissal if he did not follow through on this demand. With his characteristic brutal stubbornness, Hitler did everything he could to separate the two young people. While he only threatened to force Geli to leave Munich, he did withdraw the financial support he had been giving to her mother and other members of her family.

In summer 1928, his blackmail efforts triumphed and he succeeded in separating Geli from his chauffeur for good. Shortly afterwards, the young girl met a painter from Linz, who was so charmed by her that he immediately proposed. Hitler was informed of this by his personal police and used the same means to force his sister to oppose the union.

There is no doubting the motives that drove him to such tactics! He felt more than just a benevolent and protective friendship for his niece and was gripped by a violent feeling of jealousy, inspired by a passionate love that he did not yet dare to reveal.

I had the opportunity to see the letter in which the young, desperate suitor used his last arguments to persuade Geli to follow him. I copied it for Hitler and am therefore able to reproduce the main passages:

> 'Your uncle, aware of the influence he exerts over your mother, is now exploiting her weakness with boundless cynicism. Unfortunately, we won't be able to respond to this blackmail until you reach your majority. He is literally piling obstacles in the way of our mutual happiness. Yet he knows we are made for each other. The year of separation your mother is imposing on us before giving her consent to our union will only increase the attachment we feel for each other. My honesty finds it difficult to accept such unworthy schemes.
>
> 'However, I can only explain your uncle's attitude as essentially selfish motives that bind him to you. He simply wants you to one day belong to no one but him.'

In another passage, the young painter declares:

> 'Your uncle continues to see you as nothing but an inexperienced child and can't understand that you have become a grown-up who wants to build her own happiness. Your uncle is of a violent nature. Everyone in his Party gives way to him with the eagerness of a slave. I don't understand how his keen intelligence did not realise that his stubbornness and curious theories on marriage can only be shattered against our love and determination. He hopes to succeed in the course of this year in triumphing over us; but how little does he know your ardent soul ...'

At that time, Hitler had made up his mind to marry Geli as soon as he had achieved his political aims. In 1930 he rented an entire floor of a house at Prinz-Regenten-Platz 16, where Geli also moved to, and these years of cohabitation with her were, according to Hitler, a period of great happiness.

When he later reminisced to us of those times, he was as if transfigured. He would describe to us in great detail how the two of them would spend joyful evenings together. They did all their shopping together, went to the theatre together and regularly attended concerts. With a hint of bitterness, he would then cite Geli's minor faults: 'When I accompanied her to clothes stores, she would unpack all the hats on the shelves and demand all those in the windows to be brought to her. When she had tried on all the hats in the store, she declared she had found nothing she liked and told the saleswoman this so casually that I was embarrassed. When I whispered to Geli that she could not leave the store without buying something, after having turned it upside down, she gave me one of her disarming smiles and blurted out, "But, Uncle Adolf. Isn't that what these people are here for?'"

Hitler watched over Geli in a constant state of jealousy. Every time he went away on a propaganda tour, she had to swear a solemn oath not to take advantage of his absence to renew certain acquaintances, and it was only when she went to her mother's that he did not have her chaperoned. This lasted until September 1931. At that time, Hitler met a little saleswoman called Eva Braun in Heinrich Hoffmann's shop, who had fallen in love with him and had decided she would have him for her own. Hitler flirted with her a little, but it was nothing serious.

On 17 September 1931, Hitler called Geli at Berchtesgaden, where she was staying, telling her to come home. The next day there was a violent scene between them after he had suddenly decided to go to Nuremberg. Geli reproached her uncle for having brought her back to Munich for nothing and was furious that he had also forbidden her to go to Vienna during his absence, so that her voice could be assessed by a singing teacher. They were on bad terms when they parted the next morning. But Geli's bad mood turned to despair when, that same day, while searching through her uncle's overcoat, she discovered a declaration of love written in Eva Braun's handwriting. That evening, she committed suicide by shooting herself in the mouth with a revolver.

Hitler was urgently recalled from Nuremberg and took his niece's suicide so seriously that he was on the verge of ending his own life. Hess had great difficulty in wresting his pistol from him. For several days he ate nothing and merely paced up and down his room, wondering what had driven his niece to commit this fatal act. When he resumed the habit of eating, he could no longer swallow meat, and it was from this date that he became a complete vegetarian.

For many months Hitler refused to see friends and simply lived with the memory of Geli, keeping her room exactly as it was at the time of her death. He put flowers in there every day over the years to come, especially on birthdays. He carried the key to her bedroom with him until the war was declared. Even Geli's room at the Berghof remained closed. When he later remodelled the residence to make it more spacious, the wing where the girl's bedroom was located was left intact. Her clothes, toiletries and everything that had belonged to her remained in their place. Hitler even refused to return some of Geli's possessions or letters to her mother after she had requested them as mementos. All of Geli's correspondence was guarded with a jealous care by her uncle, and in April 1945 he ordered his adjutant Schaub to destroy it if it became clear that there was no longer any chance of him [Hitler] leaving Berlin. He had paintings made from photographs of Geli, which adorned all his apartments, in Munich, Berlin and the Berghof.

Six months after Geli's death, the Führer's friends finally succeeded in tearing him away from the solitude into which the tragedy had plunged him. One evening, Heinrich Hoffmann took him to the cinema and managed to place Eva Braun, as if by chance, next to him. Thus began a flirtation between Hitler and Eva Braun which, over the years, developed into a solid relationship. Hitler once confessed to me that he had never felt great love for Eva but had simply become accustomed to her. He once told me: 'Eva is very kind, but Geli was the only person in my life able to inspire me with real passion. I would never think of marrying Eva. The only woman I could have tied myself to for life would have been Geli.'

During a conversation in early 1945, someone referred to the three women who had attempted suicide over Hitler, namely Geli, Eva and Miss Mitford [Unity Mitford (1914–48)]. When it came to Geli, Hitler repeated: 'She was the only woman who won my heart and whom I could have married. Her death was a terrible ordeal for me. However, considering what has happened, I'm beginning to believe that it was better this way, because I could never have given her all the happiness she deserved.'

One evening, Hitler noticed a young girl in a Munich café who bore an uncanny resemblance to Geli and invited her to his table so that he could get to know her. Over the years, he made her take acting lessons, despite her lack of talent for the stage, and in the meantime his protégé led a very wild life. When Hitler found out, however, he stopped seeing her and subsidising her lifestyle altogether.

In the early years of her affair with Hitler, Eva Braun was a self-effacing and insecure young girl. The discretion with which she was able to conduct her meetings with Hitler made a very favourable impression on him. She never attended an official reception, and Hitler never mentioned her to his guests. At that time, she was not yet living at the Berghof, where Frau Raubal, the mother of the deceased Geli, had settled in as an intractable watchdog. Instead, a simple room was reserved for her at the nearby 'Platerhof', and from time to time she would come to join Hitler at the Berghof for a few hours.

Frau Raubal strongly reproached her half-brother for this affair. She showed deep disdain for Eva and, furious at not being able to separate her from Hitler, called her an intruder. She often suggested to Hitler that he marry an actress like Fräulein Sonnemann [Emma 'Emmy' Göring (née Sonnemann) (1893–1973)], who was Göring's wife. One day, she said to the Reichsmarschall, 'I envy you, Reichsmarschall, for two things. First, for marrying Fräulein Sonnemann and then, to have the services of a valet as perfect as Robert [Kropp]. It's a pity my brother didn't do as you did.'

Göring replied with a satisfied smile, 'I'd give him Robert at a pinch, but as for Emmy Sonnemann, never!'

Despite her appearance as a slender, blonde girl, Eva Braun had a lot of energy and willpower, and by bending entirely to the whims of her master, she gradually managed to strengthen her position. It was at the 1936 Party Congress that she finally won the respect of her lover. Frau Raubal had reprimanded Eva violently because she had not kept a sufficient distance during the Nuremberg rallies, but when she told her half-brother about it, to Frau Raubal's surprise, Hitler took up the cause of his friend. It is true that Eva had attempted suicide following the acrimonious reproaches she had received from Frau Raubal, and this act of desperation had so impressed Hitler that he dismissed his half-sister out of hand and installed Eva permanently at the Berghof.

It was from this moment that she officially entered the life of the Führer of the Third Reich. Hitler gave her a small villa in Munich, a car, and literally covered her with jewels and expensive dresses, while also providing her with an income that allowed her to satisfy all her whims.

Eva Braun knew how to adapt to the customs of high society. She had set her mind on becoming a lady and tried to copy the appearance of Frau Goebbels [Magda Goebbels (1901–1945)], whom she had taken as her role model. However, despite all her efforts and expense, she never succeeded in making people forget where she came from. Like thousands of other young girls, she remained someone whose only interest lay in extravagant attire and who was filled with terror at the idea that her weight might increase by a few grammes. As a result, Eva would eat very irregularly and took pills after each meal to make her throw up. Thanks to this habit, as well as the diet she imposed on herself, she had stomach problems. When she suffered from her digestive issues, Hitler would panic and take on the attitude of a schoolboy in love, stroking her hands and arms endlessly and calling her his little 'Patscherl'.

Eva had an unusual beauty. Her eyes, hazel in colour and with very long eyelashes, were striking, but she lost all her charm when she pulled one of her spiteful faces. Two heavy folds fell from the corners of her lips, making her appear terribly aged, and she was extremely irritable because the falseness of situation she was struggling with filled her with worry. She was alarmed by the idea of the various intrigues with which certain women in the Führer's entourage surrounded her, which led her to having a terrible inferiority complex. Being eager to know all the gossip, she then felt lost every time someone pointed out advances made to her lover by some of her guests.

Eva had a difficult character. Not knowing how to control herself and of an impulsive temperament, she often had outbursts of anger or fervour. She openly displayed her antipathy or sympathy for people who approached her, and was selfish, except towards her family members or close friends. The instability of her character made her frequently change the people around her, while the annoyance she felt because Hitler rarely appeared with her in public ate away at her. She would go mad at the thought that while she was condemned to wait for him in his room for an entire evening, he would be surrounded by a crowd of pretty women from whom intoxicating offers rose like the scent of incense.

She only appeared at Hitler's side when he was meeting with small groups and I noticed that on such occasions, she tried to shine by any means possible. She also persisted in imposing her point of view on all matters. At the Berghof, the guests considered her the mistress of the house. Hitler would change his guest of honour at each meal, but at the table Eva was invariably seated to his left. Upon leaving the table, Hitler always kissed her hand first and only then did he kiss the hand of the woman on his right.

During meals, Eva Braun took very little part in conversations, at least in the early years. Later, when she had gained more confidence, she would join in according to her mood at the time.

I saw her get upset every time Hitler continued to speak on one of his favourite topics instead of leaving the table once the meal was over, and would clearly show her impatience. During the war years, sure of the ascendancy she had gained over Hitler, she even dared to throw him disapproving glances or ask out loud what time it was. Hitler would then abruptly interrupt his monologues and rise from the table, apologising for his chatter.

Hitler had grown accustomed to his friend's effervescent character, but by no means deferred to her in everything. Indeed, Eva was subject to very strict instructions. For example, she was not allowed to sunbathe because her master did not like tanned skin, and she only attended dance parties in secret because Hitler abhorred dancing. An excellent sportswoman, Eva enjoyed swimming, skiing and gymnastics. She loved animals and lived surrounded by a German Shepherd, a Basset Hound and two Fox Terriers. In addition, Eva had patiently trained two blackbirds that were allowed to roam free in her apartment.

Most of her time, however, was spent on her toilette, to which she showed an unusual dedication. She made a binder where all her dresses were reproduced and numbered with the corresponding fabric sample, which also gave her a quick overview of her wardrobe. The sense of order with which Eva looked after all matters that affected her personally was absolutely remarkable. Hitler appreciated this quality, saying of her that she was perfectly clean and that he had never had reason to reproach her for the slightest negligence.

Eva was a regular visitor to the theatre and cinema. Hitler

always asked her opinion on the plays she had seen, although he was often misled because Eva did not judge the performances according to their real value, but according to way in which she had been received by the artists. I never saw her read a book that was even slightly serious. She only enjoyed detective novels and modern literature, which corresponded to the level of her intellectual education.

By early 1938, Miss Mitford had managed to meet Hitler more frequently than was usual. Eva Braun was horrified and staged a second suicide attempt, which brought her contrite lover back to her. From then on, her position was definitively established. Hitler was frightened by the thought that she might try it again one day and that a public scandal would break out. In any case, I had the very clear impression that from that moment on, Eva was firmly in place. She increasingly asserted her personality in society and was given more respectful consideration.

Every year she was allowed to take friends on holiday to Italy, and from time to time was also allowed to make an appearance in Berlin, where she was less visible than at the Berghof. Hitler did not forbid her from walking around Berlin, going shopping, visiting her hairdresser or her dressmaker, and even allowed her to follow the theatre season, although on all these occasions, she had to remain anonymous.

The marriage of her sister Gretel to Hermann Fegelein, Himmler's personal representative to the Führer, marked a further step in Eva's emancipation. From then on, she was presented to the outside world as Fegelein's sister-in-law and showed a genuine attachment to her brother-in-law. However, she failed to save his skin when Hitler had him executed during Berlin's final days.

At the beginning of 1945 she told me: 'Don't you think I've become much freer? Before, I didn't know what attitude to take during official receptions, but now I am someone: I'm the sister-in-law of Gruppenführer Fegelein. He introduces me to a lot of people I never knew, and now I also know a lot of things I had no idea about before.'

Eva's two visits to Berlin in early 1945 had left her very disappointed. Hitler, who had been following an even stricter vegetarian diet for a year, demanded that she join him in it. 'We argue about it every day,' she complained. 'Once and for all, I can't swallow the horrible mixtures he delights in. I also think the whole atmosphere here has changed. I was so looking forward to joining him in Berlin, but now I'm starting to regret it. Adolf only talks to me about his food and dogs. That wretched pest Blondi [Hitler's favourite German Shepherd] drives me crazy. Sometimes I kick her under the table and Adolf gets all anxious when the beast panics. It's my way of getting revenge.'

It can be said that when it came to politics, Eva was completely ignorant and careless. When she saw from the dismayed faces of Hitler's associates and secretaries that something abnormal had just happened, she would pester us to find out why.

She often complained that no one kept her informed of events. When someone explained some unpleasant news to her, she always exclaimed with a candid air: 'But, my children, I know absolutely nothing about these horrors.'

The day after certain receptions, she would often confess to me: 'Fegelein introduced me to men who told me such curious stories that I couldn't believe my ears. It was like I was transported to another world.' Before immediately adding: 'In the end, isn't it better that I don't know what's happening elsewhere? After all, I can't do anything about it.' And so she absolved herself of responsibility with the carelessness of a child, although she was always in a good mood again after saying such things. She would then encourage us to drink and enjoy life and, in a supreme challenge to the established order, even dared to smoke a cigarette. However, after this gesture of revolt, she made sure to gargle carefully before returning to her suspicious lover.

Furthermore, she realised what awaited her the day Germany collapsed, knowing there was no chance she would survive such a disaster. In April 1945 she confessed to me: 'If we lose this war, and I'm beginning to believe we will, despite Adolf's optimism, I know what awaits me, but I've come to terms with it.' Hitler's determination to send her to Berchtesgaden before the capital was completely destroyed, gave way due to her fierce resolve to stay close to him, 'to be with him to the end'. In her last letter to her sister, Gretl Fegelein, dated 23 April 1945, which I took with me, she wrote these exact words: 'Every day and every hour we wait for the end. But there's no question of us falling into enemy hands alive.'

Unlike the Führer, Eva Braun was very superstitious. All her lingerie was embroidered with a monogram in which her initials formed a stylised four-leafed clover. In this way Eva acknowledged the incredible luck that had favoured her in having been chosen among so many others by the all-powerful man of the Reich. After a long affair, this chance allowed her to enter into history by marrying the man in her life, the very day before their common end. This funereal marriage, on the threshold of nothingness, constituted the crowning and apotheosis of her life as a dull little courtesan.

[illegible]

VII

In politics, you need the support of women;
then men follow you on their own.

Hitler

Hitler was always perfectly natural in his attentiveness and cordiality towards women. His gallant manners, marked by an 'old Austrian' accent, exercised an undeniable charm over them, and he treated his female staff with great respect and without prejudice. He certainly demanded a lot from them, including the almost total sacrifice of their freedom, but on the other hand, he knew how to recognise the true value of their work, paid them generously and, in the event of illness, always showed his concern. With us, his secretaries, he was always extremely polite, always rose from his chair to greet us, and always showed us the same respect he displayed in more worldly company. When we stayed with him at the Berghof, he would lead us to the table when it was our turn, just as he did with his distinguished guests.

During his many travels throughout Germany, he had become so accustomed to the presence of his secretaries that, just as in Berlin, he regularly used to invite us to his 5 o'clock teas. During moments of relaxation, he would come and chat in the small room reserved for us in his apartment in the Reich Chancellery. It was a real all-purpose room: we wrote our letters there, ate our meals together there when we were not invited elsewhere, we mended our stockings there and … we waited there. It was furnished in a very motley manner. There was a sofa, a small, white-painted wardrobe, a desk, a few armchairs and a huge octagonal table that got in everyone's way. However, Hitler felt very comfortable there and would come to take refuge every time he wanted to contemplate something and take a moment's rest.

The Führer was very sensitive to feminine beauty, but in his enthusiasm, he readily attributed certain qualities of character and external charm that were not always justified. He would see an imaginary talent in the beauty of certain women, but when his mistakes were pointed out, such criticism had no effect on his stubbornness in attributing to those pretty women around him an entirely imaginary intelligence and culture. Consequently, young, good-looking people would find themselves taking artistic training courses at his expense that would last for years, but without any results!

Hitler was a poor psychologist when it came to women because, being a consummate actor himself, he had difficulty distinguishing between what was natural and what was not. Everyone who approached him, especially women, tried to show themselves off as best they could, and so Hitler, too, often took their eagerness and hypocritical behaviour at face value. He had a marked predilection for one of his secretaries, although it is true that she was always in a sunny mood, agreed with him on everything and knew how to flatter his vanity admirably. Hitler would always brighten up in her presence and his conversation would suddenly burst with witty remarks.

Hitler had no concept of matters of the heart and soul. He did not understand, for example, that in a marriage the two spouses need to have an affinity in both personality and opinions. For him, the ideal couple was judged solely on physical appearances, and he believed that a marriage with a pretty, healthy woman would automatically be a happy one. As with all the unions he arranged, he was inspired only by these considerations, even though it turned out that his predictions of happiness were often contradicted by the facts. One day I drew his attention to the increasing number of divorces occurring among the ranks of leading Party men, under the false pretext that their wives had failed to adapt to their husbands' new social situation. I explained to him that the population was severely critical of this veritable epidemic of divorces and that the Party's reputation was suffering as a result.

Hitler retorted sharply: 'In my opinion, by right, the prettiest women belong to the best soldiers.' This proves that he judged humanity and in particular the problem of the sexes purely from a material angle …

I previously said that he had not married because having a family, with all the responsibilities it entails, would have created too many obstacles in his career and in his struggles. He also admitted to me that his marriage would have made him lose a great deal of the sympathy and prestige he prided himself on having among his female voters. 'My influence on the female population of the Reich increased purely because I have not become a one-woman

man. I could never have allowed myself to lose my popularity among German women, because they represent too important an element in election campaigns.' In saying this, Hitler revealed himself, once again, to be shamelessly calculating and a man ready to sacrifice everything to achieve his goal.

It is true that many women fell passionately in love with him, while others were obsessed with him fathering a child with them. One day, a young girl managed to gain access to his apartment in Munich, and when she found herself in his presence, she tore off her bodice in a great gesture of passionate frenzy.

From that day on, Hitler no longer met unknown women to whom he had granted an interview alone, fearing that these tête-à-têtes might compromise him in some scandalous affair. He was haunted by the fear that a woman might spread vicious rumours that went against his reputation as a decent man. It is this obsession that explains the discreet way in which he knew how to circumscribe his lovers. He would maintain an absolute silence around us about his relationships and was also very careful in choosing his guests, even for official receptions. When he learned, for example, that an actress was exploiting for her own personal gain the honour he had done her by inviting her to a party, he publicly denounced her and had the impudent woman placed on a blacklist. Now she would never appear at one of his receptions!

For many years I had the opportunity to observe Hitler's habits and actions as objectively as possible. In all sincerity, I believe I can refute the accusations that he had an abnormal sex life. With his exclusively vegetarian diet, his refusal to take any alcoholic stimulant and his intense work ethic, I believe it would have been difficult for him to indulge in abuse. I am convinced that in this area he was perfectly normal. On the contrary, I often had the impression that he was forcing himself not to be enticed by the charms of one or other of the artists that he used to meet.

He was deeply attached to Eva Braun for twelve years. I have already said that he had been favourably impressed, at the beginning of their relationship, by the absolute discretion with which she conducted herself around him, even though the young girl's rather delicate constitution and blonde hair did not correspond at all to his physical ideals. He preferred the type of women from southern Germany: dark-haired, robust and with a natural complexion.

Hitler acknowledged in his interviews that women had played an important role in his political career and he would systematically flatter the tastes and instincts of female voters during his election campaigns. From the beginning, women had been enthusiastic admirers of his fiery proselytising. I know he received countless parcels and letters from unknown women during his imprisonment in Landsberg. Every time he had found himself faced with insurmountable difficulties during his eventful career, women had helped him out of trouble. He liked to give us the following example:

'One day, I accepted a loan of 40,000 MK on behalf of the Party. To my dismay, the cashflow I'd consequently expected didn't materialise. The coffers were horribly empty and as the deadline approached, I still didn't know how to honour my promise. I even considered committing suicide so as not to live through the shame. Four days before the fateful date, I expressed my distress to Frau Bruckmann,[1] who immediately began campaigning on my behalf. The next day, Herr Kierdorf, the president of the Union Charbonnière, asked me to come to his house. At his request, I explained my agenda to him in detail, the timeliness of which struck him. I thus gained an important follower of the National Socialist movement but, what is more, he also asked me to accept the sum in question and thus enabled me to pay off my debts in due time.'

Hitler believed the Third Reich had produced four superior women. First there was Frau Scholtz-Klinck, the talented organiser of the Nazi women's movement. Then Frau Wagner, who had succeeded in recreating in Bayreuth the mystical atmosphere of the works of the brilliant composer. Then came Frau Troost, in whom he admired the artistic assurance with which she had continued the work of her late husband. When Hitler moved into his apartment in Munich, Frau Bruckmann took him to the studios of the architect Troost, who had created a new style of furnishing. On this occasion Troost showed him the plans he had drawn up for the reconstruction of the Glass Palace in Munich, which had not been accepted by the jury. Hitler was enthusiastic about these projects and had them realised during the construction of the 'House of German Art' in Munich. Troost was also the architect of the 'Brown House' in Munich and part of the Reich Chancellery in Berlin. Hitler called Troost 'professor', and this honorary title was transferred to his wife after his [Troost's] death. Frau Troost later had a major influence on Hitler's artistic tastes, managing to make him share her personal conception of the harmony of colours. She alone was responsible for decorating Hitler's residences in Berlin, Munich and the Berghof. Only his private apartment in Munich retained its old-fashioned charm from the time when he had spent his happiest years there in the company of his niece, Geli Raubal.

The fourth woman for whom Hitler had special admiration was Leni Riefenstahl, considering her to be a remarkable actress and a film producer of real talent. The world's press was excited by the reports that came from the Führer's enthusiasm for the young filmmaker, and it is true that Eva hated Leni's femininity. However, as it is only results that count, was it not Eva who finally triumphed over the 'Pompadour' by sealing her union with the Reich's touchy bachelor in a marriage marked with the seal of death?

VIII

Man has a natural tendency to be ungrateful.

Hitler

It must be noted that Hitler, who in everyday life could be surprisingly stingy when it came to detail, always knew how to show gratitude to those who had done him a favour, and on such occasions could be remarkably generous. The explanation for this generosity is not due purely to his concern to carve out for himself a reputation as a generous and grateful man, but the actual gesture of giving and rewarding gave him genuine pleasure and satisfaction.

In the years following his seizure of power, he was still in the habit of personally choosing every gift he intended to give, and on more than one occasion I saw him thinking hard to guess what might please a person. He kept repeating to me like a leitmotif: 'I know how much ingratitude hurts, and it's so easy to show gratitude.'

This eagerness with which Hitler rewarded even the smallest bit of personal service and the zeal with which his wishes were met became a real source of profit for the beneficiaries. A kind of bidding war soon existed among some of his colleagues as to who could offer him small gifts on the most varied of occasions. Very often, these gestures were inspired only by a cold calculation of seeing them returned a hundredfold. The custom of giving each other gifts in this way had received official recognition in the Third Reich.

Göring knew how to exploit this state of affairs admirably. The determination with which he sought honorary presidencies of the most improbable associations and unions, ranging from the presidency of the goldsmiths to the position of the Reich Master of the Hounds, cannot be explained by his excessive vanity alone, but also by the noble gifts these positions brought him. Hitler was far from having the same luxurious tastes he tolerated in Göring. Instead, he was completely happy and satisfied when he could rest in his Munich apartment, which until the end of the war was filled with bric-a-brac furniture bought during the years he was fighting for power. He used to say: 'I feel really at home in Munich. Wherever I look, the smallest piece of furniture, the smallest painting, even the linen, evoke memories of struggle, of deprivation, but also of happiness. I bought all the furniture with my savings, little by little, and often second-hand. My niece Geli accompanied me and that's not the least of the reasons why my heart remains attached to her.'

Hitler adored children. In his early years in power, his pockets were always stuffed with chocolate, which he distributed with radiant joy to the crowds of children who had come to see 'Herr Hitler'. I cannot say to what extent these distributions of sweets were inspired by cheap propaganda, but I am convinced it responded in part to the affectionate friendship he had for young people. As in everything Hitler did, we must recognise the dual tendencies. Good and bad, true and false, the ideal and materialism were all so intensely combined within him that it was very difficult to distinguish between virtue and vice. Only the initiated took part in the diabolical game by which he knew how to keep face in the most compromising circumstances, so consummate was his skill.

Hitler was a very bad psychologist. While the outward appearance of a woman – a slender figure and a pretty dress – a hard and determined air in a man, or a soldier's demeanour always made an impression on him, when it came to children, his judgements were often found wanting.

I would like to illustrate Hitler's curious misadventures with the story of little Berneudi, a 5-year-old girl with huge blue eyes and abundant blonde hair, whom he noticed one day in a crowd of children who had come to greet him at the Berghof. He became so fond of the little girl that he encouraged her to come and see him whenever she could. For three years, her mother knew how to put herself in the spotlight, introducing her little girl to Hitler on every different occasion. Hitler always treated the little girl with fatherly kindness and was photographed with her several times. One day, an anonymous letter arrived and abruptly put an end to these joyful encounters, after denouncing the girl's mother to be half-Jewish. Genuinely upset, Hitler informed her not to try to approach him again and had all the photographs showing him playing with little Berneudi destroyed. The incident affected him greatly, brutally reminding him once again of the solitude he lived in, a solitude that weighed terribly on him because it violated those natural feelings that were deeply anchored in him.

During his years in power, Hitler took pleasure in lighting the candles on a Christmas tree at Christmastime. The sweetness of family joys was like a physical need for him, and yet he was never to realise his attachment to children by getting married. True happiness at home was unknown to him. The only women in his life, with the exception of a few flings and his affair with Eva Braun, were the wives of other men. He only mixed with children – other people's children – with a naive enthusiasm. Hitler was a repressed person in affection, in family joy, in everything that creates happiness in the natural cell of society, and he suffered for it. This unsatisfied soul, who refused to indulge in natural and simple happiness, was constantly searching for balance in life. In his isolation, he created a dream world for himself that ignored all the noble feelings of humanity, and this constant worry and emotional instability quickly turned into indifference, followed by amorality. Towards the end, Hitler was nothing more than a monster of cruelty and despotism.

With the ideas of family and filial affection being absolutely foreign to him, it is unsurprising that he coldly sent millions of young people to their deaths, for the sole satisfaction of sacrificing them to the mission he believed himself invested in. The death of a human being left him completely unmoved. He saw humanity merely as a long chain of men, with himself as the initial link. In his eyes, children were nothing more than the means to allow one to expect an expanded living space. Rejecting any philosophical concept of the afterlife, he considered it completely normal that the ashes of bodies cremated in concentration camps were used to fertilise the vegetable gardens in which the SS hordes grew their provisions.

However, Hitler was not always able to control his natural impulses. There were times when he anxiously sought to cling on to something that could give him the inner peace that all men need in order to be happy.

We often discussed childhood memories during our endless fireside chats. When he spoke, I felt the chord of happiness vibrate within him, the complete happiness he had known in his humble home, surrounded by his mother's love. It was in the evocation of his youth that he would take refuge in his moments of isolation.

Another happy period of his life corresponded to the years of struggle that preceded his accession to power. He had no time to think back then, as he pursued his supreme goal with unparalleled tenacity. He was completely absorbed in his mission but never felt the need to seek out any form of psychological balance. However, he did have devoted companions at his side during these years, true friends, not lemmings or profiteers who were always on the lookout for a beneficial situation. At that time, his team, aspiring body and soul to the same ideal, shared all his sorrows, his setbacks and his joys.

Hence the extraordinary loyalty that Hitler maintained for so long from his first companions. Among these men, most of them rough, but steeped in the harsh school of subversive political activity, he found a moral refuge. Some of them had been intoxicated by the extraordinary successes they had experienced, while others had been unable to adapt to change or bear the heavy responsibilities that later fell upon them. Others would betray him and become his enemies, although one is always struck by the fact that the men who surrounded him were below average.

This did not prevent Weber, Graf and even Maurice [Christian(?) Weber (1883–1945), Ulrich Graf (1878–1950), Emil Maurice (1897–1972)] from addressing him informally. Hamann [Joachim(?) Hamann (1913–1945)] and Hoffmann simply called him 'Herr Hitler'. In his state of neuropathic anxiety and mental instability, these men seemed like a lifeline to him, to which he could cling in moments of despondency. The loyalty and camaraderie of his early companions were a vigorous tonic to him; hence the leniency with which Hitler judged the most serious atrocities committed by his protégés.

I will only cite the example of Streicher [Julius Streicher (1885–1946)], whom he had to dismiss when he learned that the latter had had a solid gold box made for his friend using rings collected to replenish Germany's war coffers. Hitler was upset by the measures he had been forced to take and, years later, thought about wiping the slate clean and rehabilitating the Gauleiter of Franconia.

The same was true for Schaub. Schaub had become Hitler's adjutant through Bormann, when the latter succeeded in disgracing Hitler's former adjutant, Brückner. Schaub was a founding member of the Nazi movement. Hitler often told us how, early in his agitator days, he was struck by a man who faithfully attended all his meetings and limped along to all his parades. A sincere friendship was to blossom from these initial meetings, especially when Schaub was imprisoned at Landsberg alongside Hitler, who made Schaub his factotum after his release. Schaub was not only responsible for the Führer's personal affairs, but soon became his confidant in the most secret state matters. His duties included keeping Hitler informed about cinema and theatre programmes, arranging his private visits, making payments from his cheque book, organising his private documents, ensuring originals of all international agreements and important memoranda written by Hitler were kept in his safe, as well as carrying out the most confidential procedures for him.

It can be said that Schaub enjoyed unlimited confidence in the eyes of his master. However, his unstable and calculating character meant he unfortunately took advantage of his privileged situation to carry out minor schemes and to satisfy personal grudges. Knowing Hitler was fond of the 'scandalous tittle-tattle' surrounding his General Staff, Schaub made it his duty to inform Hitler of all the little incidents in which the people around him were involved. Hitler listened to the gossip with an interested ear and often took disciplinary measures that were completely disproportionate to the trivial acts of which his associates were guilty.

As a consequence of this, Schaub was universally hated, but no one dared to confront him publicly because of his pernicious influence on the Führer, even though the latter was unaware that Schaub's guilty pleasure was alcohol. Yet, if he admitted, for example, that he had taken a Berlin prostitute as a girlfriend, then Hitler found it difficult to forgive his hedonism. When it was reported to him that his adjutant had caused a scandal after being completely drunk at various receptions, Hitler could only flap his arms in despair and invariably reply: 'I know his faults. It's sad, but what do you want me to do? He's all I have; there's no one to replace him.'

Hitler's quarrels with Ley [Robert Ley (1890–1945)] are the stuff of theatre. In Hitler's eyes, the leader of the German Labour Front was a brilliant organiser and a great idealist with fantastic ideas, and he always spoke with admiration of Ley's social work, which was carried out in support of the working class. Nevertheless, Hitler knew Ley was far from being a saint. Even in the years when Ley's conduct became increasingly scandalous and the articles he published in the press irritated even the Party leaders, Hitler would not be swayed and argued that a certain section of the population needed Ley's literature.

When Frau Igne Ley was still alive, Hitler was her frequent guest. He found her remarkably beautiful and considered her to be her husband's better angel, convinced as he was that she had almost succeeded in making him lose the habit of drinking and smoking to excess. However, everyone knew that these two vices, pushed to the extreme, continued to wreak havoc on Ley. Even to this day I cannot understand how Hitler could have believed that this inveterate drunkard could have changed his deplorable habits under the fortunate influence of his wife.

Hitler enjoyed the artistic environment he found among the

Leys, which was to be expected considering Frau Ley came from an ancient family of artists. The young woman's suicide affected Hitler deeply. His break with the Goebbels household and the death of Frau Ley deprived him of the pleasure of occasionally immersing himself in an atmosphere that was a change from the evenings spent by the fireside.

Ley was ridiculously in love with his wife and acted like a peacock whenever he was in her presence, permanently showing off his tail in front of his beloved. One day when he was escorting me to the table at the Berghof, he said to me, stammering with emotion and pointing to his wife, who was in front of him on Hitler's arm: 'Isn't she beautiful, isn't she radiant?' I could barely suppress a burst of laughter at the absurdity of such vanity.

I tell this story to show how attached Ley was to his wife, how he showed his passion for her, and to explain why his attitude after her death became a source of consternation for everyone, including Hitler. The Führer was outraged when he learned that Ley had taken up with a 19-year-old Estonian dancer, whose main virtue was that she reminded him of his wife. Dr Morell had been instructed to show us photographs of the ballerina, in which a striking resemblance was indeed observed. At Ley's insistence, her hair, make-up and attire were so identical to Frau Ley's that you would look at her and think you were hallucinating. I must add, however, that the young Estonian far surpassed Frau Ley in intelligence and skill. Ley had thought to gain Hitler's indulgence by emphasising his young protégée's resemblance to his late wife, in the hope of obtaining his permission to marry her. But his efforts were in vain. Hitler considered this cult, which consisted of reviving the deceased in the guise of another woman, as an insult to the dead's memory. Consequently, he told me that he would never set foot in Ley's home again.

All things considered, I believe that Hitler had only one great friend who had any real influence on him, and that was the poet Eckhart [Dietrich Eckhart (1868–1923)]. One may wonder how Hitler, after 1918, was able to access circles which, normally, would have been closed to the First World War corporal. Many people are unaware that he met Eckhart in 1920. It so happened that the poet attended a meeting of officials of the nascent NSDAP. Hitler, with his customary passion, spoke of the chaotic situation in which Germany found itself and urged the population to make an effort at recovery, drawing inspiration from the new National Socialist doctrine. The magnetism he exuded, his lapidary arguments, his passionate eloquence, deeply struck the old patriotic poet. Eckhart was genuinely thrilled, telling Hitler 'straight away' that he considered him the man the whole world would soon be talking about. He immediately set about campaigning to win the sympathy of the Munich salons for the cause. He introduced him to industrialists, senior officials, artists, and he proselytised tirelessly to rally Bavarian nationalists to the National Socialist movement. Eckhart fought firmly against the prejudices of certain circles who did not accept that an ex-corporal, without position or references, could put himself at the head of a movement whose aim was to create a spiritually united Germany. He did not shy away from any sacrifice that might reduce the hesitation of financial and economic circles in the face of the 'unknown newcomer' who posed as the country's liberator. The poet became a real source of income for the new party, tirelessly organising collections and allowing the early, limited propaganda to unfold into fully organised campaigns.

But this material help was small when compared to the direct influence Eckhart exercised on his admirer. Hitler regarded the poet, who was twenty years his senior, as his benefactor and his sincerest friend. His vast knowledge, sparkling humour and penetrating intelligence impressed him to the point that, touchy as Hitler was on the subject, he considered himself his disciple. They were true friends. Eckhart's influence was undoubtedly decisive on Hitler's personality and character, saving him from many disappointments and painful trials and errors in his early career.

When Eckhart's adaptation of a play by Henrik Ibsen was performed, it meant travelling frequently to Berlin. Hitler accompanied the poet every time and thus had the opportunity to infiltrate the upper middle-class circles of Berlin, which were even more resistant to his ideas than those in Munich. Through his friend, Hitler subsequently made contact with well-known writers, respected economists and renowned artists.

Eckhart's death was a severe blow to Hitler. Never again in his life was he given the chance to find a friend with whom he would live in such harmony of thought and feeling. Every time he spoke to me about the poet, his eyes would mist over. After taking power, Hitler often repeated that he regretted the premature death of the great writer all the more because it would finally have been possible to repay him for the favours he had shown him.

However, if I said at the beginning of this chapter that Hitler showed absolute loyalty to his first comrades, this recognition complex vanished during the last years of his life due to various circumstances. I knew many men, especially generals, to whom he had shown signs of friendship for many years and who suddenly fell into oblivion. Many of his early friends incurred his wrath, and no plausible explanation could be given for this change in attitude. I would particularly like to cite the example of Dr Brandt, who, since 1933, had accompanied Hitler on all his travels.

It is interesting to recall how this young doctor had entered the Führer's good graces, especially when Hitler would later display all the ingratitude and hatred he was capable of when someone lost his confidence.

When Hitler and his early followers were imprisoned in Landsberg, the latter spent their time in trivial correspondence, while their master wrote the National Socialist bible *Mein Kampf*. His first chauffeur, Emil Maurice, sent a letter of admiration to Anni Rehborn, who at the time was the world swimming champion, and a regular correspondence ensued. When Hitler left prison, his driver introduced him to the sportswoman and the two became friends. One day, she introduced him to her fiancé, a young assistant physician from Bochum called Karl Brandt.

At that time, Hitler was still in the habit of driving around the German countryside at breakneck speed and it was during one of these trips that he had an accident in which his adjutant,

Brückner, was seriously injured. As chance would have it, Dr Brandt and Fräulein Rehborn were there, and the skill with which Brandt gave first aid to the wounded man using only makeshift equipment attracted Hitler's sympathetic attention, and he immediately appointed him as his personal physician. Brandt eagerly accepted and continued his studies at the University of Berlin, graduating as a surgeon of great renown. However, the peace between the Führer of the Third Reich and his personal physician was disturbed when Dr Morell appeared and was appointed Hitler's doctor.

Brandt rejected Morell's healing methods and practically called him a charlatan in public, joking about the 'dodgy' doctor's vanity and lust for profit. There were not only heated altercations between Brandt and Morell, but also violent scenes between Hitler and Brandt due to the fact Morell was quick to report to his master all the disparaging remarks made against him. Hitler was at the mercy of the treatment Morell imposed on him and lent too lenient an ear to his gossip. In an effort to put an end to the intrigues, he instead gave the two rivals the title of professor.

During the war, Hitler had less and less recourse to Brandt's care, who was now only concerned with the medical supplies of the troops on the Eastern Front. Appointed Commissioner of Health and Public Services for the entire Reich, it was in this capacity that he carried out the research and experiments for which he was so violently criticised at Nuremberg.

However, at this time Brandt was still on relatively good terms with Hitler, who frequently summoned him to private meetings, which did not fail to attract the hatred and distrust of Bormann. The most sordid schemes were staged to detach Hitler from Brandt, who unfortunately, was too upright in character not to fall into the underhand and spiteful traps that surrounded him.

Brandt was keen to warn Hitler against Morell's treatments. One day he summoned the Führer's closest colleagues and explained to them that Hitler's failing health could no longer be left in the hands of such a charlatan. In September 1944 Hitler himself made a violent scene when Brandt advised him to seek treatment from well-known luminaries at the Academy. When Brandt demonstrated to him that some of the pills Morell was making him take contained a strong poison, Hitler turned his back on him completely and dismissed him.

The sympathy Hitler had always shown for Brandt had changed into such blind hatred that he was convinced it was Brandt who intended to poison him. To him, the rivalry between his two doctors was proof that Brandt was part of a band of conspirators who were determined to get rid of him. His hatred would only grow in the last months of the war. In March 1945, he learned that Brandt had sent his wife to western Germany, to a region that was about to be occupied by the Allies. Interpreting this gesture as an act of high treason, Hitler had Brandt sentenced to death, but the arrival of the American troops saved him from execution. Yet his death was only postponed and by condemning Brandt to hang, the Nuremberg court gave Hitler posthumous satisfaction.

IX

It is only one step from dignity to ridicule.

Hitler

From what we have discussed it is clear that Hitler had two means of success developed to an almost genius degree: his will and his memory. It is all the more curious to note that his fierce harshness and stubbornness were combined with another trait of his character that was all about flexibility and cunning.

If Hitler was a monster of will and a mnemonic genius, he was also, and I would almost dare say above all, a master of pantomime and hypocrisy. Indeed, of such natural hypocrisy that even he fell for it, which at the same time was also so calculated that it inspired each of his gestures and actions.

Hitler was inculcated with the axiom that appears at the top of this page. He quoted it frequently during our exchanges and explained to me that he had made it a principle never to lose face in front of those to whom he was speaking, or in the eyes of those around him. He often paraphrased it by quoting the popular old proverb which states that 'no man is a hero to his valet'.

With consummate art, and with a jealous concern not to tarnish the brilliance of his aura, Hitler knew how to create a mask for himself in all situations. This fear of making a mistake was literally a pathological one and explains the duplicity he displayed in countless circumstances. Later, I will emphasise the difficulties that Morell, his personal physician, experienced in getting him to accept the idea of having a massage or an X-ray. Hitler was obsessed with the embarrassment of undressing in front of a stranger, for fear that the latter might take advantage of it, to the detriment of his reputation. Moreover, his valet was never allowed to enter until Hitler was dressed from head to toe. This concern for 'what people will say' was evident in the smallest details. For example, after taking power, Hitler no longer wore the famous leather trousers used in Bavaria. He regretted no longer being able to make himself so comfortable, but, he said, 'To wear such shorts trousers, you must have tanned knees, which I don't.' As the head of state, he was simply afraid of looking ridiculous in such an outfit.

As a matter of principle, he also avoided corresponding with any of his female acquaintances. One day, a love letter written by Streicher fell into prying hands, and the contents were so fiery that the Gauleiter of Franconia became a public laughing stock. On top of this, Hitler also believed that great men should not write love letters. He obviously corresponded with his friend Eva, but I know his letters were always written in very brief terms and never contained any sentimental outpourings. They were personally handed over to their recipient by Bormann, Schaub or Fegelein, and were never entrusted to the post office.

Hitler paid particular attention to the organisation of his parties. He was terrified that his staff might make mistakes in front of his guests, mistakes that would tarnish the lustre of his prestige. I once heard him threaten Kallenberg, his butler, with the worst punishments if any mishaps occurred during the evening. He used to gather the staff together before each function to remind them of the importance of their role, and before the guests arrived, he always checked the table himself, to see if anything had been forgotten. On Ribbentrop's return from Moscow in 1939, he questioned the orderly officer who had accompanied him in depth. When the officer informed him that Stalin had inspected the table at length to ensure nothing was missing before calling upon his guests, I was imprudent enough to remark: 'Stalin seems to have the same concern for impeccable presentation as you do,' only to draw the irate response: '*My* servants and *my* home are always perfect!'

I could cite countless examples of Hitler's obsession with avoiding any damage being done to his reputation, but the following episode is so characteristic that I cannot help but mention it.

Before taking power, he was given a Scottish Terrier that he had taken a liking to. The little dog's cuddly demeanour clearly amused him. 'Burli', that was her name, had the run of the house; she sprawled on the armchairs and chewed on top secret documents. Hitler played with her as if she was a child but was careful to indulge in such actions only when out of sight of any outsiders. Even in front of me, he would send the animal away roughly when it approached, only to call it back, with the sweetest words, as soon as I had left the room. He had forbidden Hoffmann, his photographer, to publish a photograph showing him playing with Burli, explaining gravely that a man in his position could only appear in public with a sheepdog at his side.

If Hitler was scrupulously careful about his outward appearances, he took the same care with his reputation, which he wanted to remain unblemished at all costs. Under no circumstances would he have compromised his good name to settle disputes or arbitrate rivalries. His sense of responsibility was very flexible. With a cunning that bordered on cynicism, he knew how to exonerate himself in the most compromising situations.

I have seen him operate like this with a complete lack of scruples. He who knew everything, who was aware of everything, often remained hidden in the shadows so as not to diminish himself when faced with thorny dilemmas. He knew how to use scapegoats, not to mention the most bogus pretexts to conceal the deep reasons for his actions and to ward off any compromise where he might have risked getting into trouble.

When he wanted to get rid of someone, he rarely admitted his real motives, but always used pretexts to mislead everyone. I will only cite the example of Field Marshal von Blomberg [Werner von Blomberg (1878–1946)], who was a victim of the most shameful of stratagems and consequently had to abandon his post as head of the Wehrmacht.

When von Blomberg informed Hitler of his intention to marry his secretary, Hitler had suddenly found a perfect pretext to expel him from his post, believing him to be thwarting his plans for organising the Reich. The Führer gave his consent to the marriage and, alongside Göring, even acted as witness. You can imagine von Blomberg's surprise when a Gestapo report was quickly produced detailing his young wife's dubious past and ordering him to leave the army. Hitler had planned everything, even von Blomberg's acceptance of the divorce, which would have upset his plans. The letter demanding his resignation also stipulated that he could only return to his former position after a one-year stay abroad.

A few months after this event, the Wehrmacht, under Hitler's direct orders, rushed into Austria. I am convinced that this affair was completely fabricated to allow Hitler to carry out his plan to invade Austria, a plan that von Blomberg had dared to speak out against.

In another case of incongruity – this time concerning Captain Albrecht [Alwin-Broder Albrecht (1903–45)], his naval adviser – the Commander of the German Fleet had reservations about the captain's marriage with a young girl from the lower middle class. Hitler, against the advice of his Grand Admiral, nevertheless gave his approval, thus proving that if he had not had an ulterior motive, he could also have supported Field Marshal von Blomberg.

This incident was often spoken of during the fireside chats. Hitler, however, always abdicated responsibility and instead blamed von Blomberg's forced departure on the intransigence of the officer class of the Wehrmacht General Staff. Yet it is rather curious that after the failed assassination attempt of 20 July 1944, Hitler brought up the von Blomberg case again. Now, he furiously blamed the officers of the General Staff for all the setbacks suffered by the army and, as proof of their criminal duplicity, cited the fact that they should have reported von Blomberg's liaison to him before the marriage ceremony and not afterwards, when it was too late.

When frictions and rivalries broke out between Party leaders, Hitler never took sides and instead withdrew into an attitude of benevolent neutrality towards the antagonists, while closely monitoring the development of events. I often had the impression that the rivalries for influence between Hess and Göring, Göring and Himmler, Goebbels and Göring, Goebbels and Ribbentrop, etc., were of great amusement to him. However, if he found that affairs of state were suffering because of these rivalries, he gave free rein to his discontent, castigating his lieutenants' attitudes in the most violent terms. I once asked him why he did not arbitrate these fights from the very beginning, to nip them in the bud. He answered evasively: 'Let the gentlemen sort it out among themselves. I've better things to do than get involved in their affairs.'

The truth is that his attitude only served to stir up these rivalries, his tacit aim being to prevent his lieutenants from forming a united front which could have rebelled against his despotism.

It was curious to see how Hitler was able to evade responsibility when people managed to approach him to appeal for clemency. He rarely behaved like an uncompromising dictator in the presence of the victims. Quite simply, he lacked the courage to defend legislation that he himself had enacted. He regularly promised to intervene, and, in many cases, actually corrected certain errors of justice or abuses. Such gestures explain why the myth spread among the German people that Hitler was unaware of his regime's atrocities.

I said during a conversation one day how, very often, people who had been wrongly attacked would cry out in their despair: 'If the Führer knew about these injustices, he wouldn't tolerate them.' However, Hitler stared at me with an icy look and blurted out the words: 'This is nonsense. I know everything.'

This was proof that all his interventions and all the exceptions he granted certain people were not inspired by a feeling of mercy, but only served to hide his natural ruthlessness.

Hitler made life difficult for himself with his lack of openness. I will cite merely the example of a kitchen assistant whom Morell had hired in 1943 to prepare the vegetarian meals that by then made up the Führer's exclusive diet. For six months, Hitler was full of praise for the new recruit's culinary skills and even invited her to have tea with us from time to time. One day, the Gestapo learned that the woman's family tree did not conform to the code of the perfect Aryan. Having Hitler's meal prepared by a 'quarter Jew' was impossible! Yet Hitler did not dismiss her immediately. As usual, he first played a horrible joke on her by saying that he had stomach problems and therefore hardly touched the food she had prepared. The cook was in despair and could not explain this sudden lack of appetite. Hitler maintained his silence on the matter and waited until February 1944 to put an end to the story. Departing for a long stay in Berchtesgaden, he gave his cook leave for the same period, still not daring to admit the reason for his strange behaviour. Instead, it was Bormann who, by letter, asked the cook to consider herself dismissed from Hitler's personal service because of her racial background. But the case was far from closed! The cook managed to see Hitler again and complained that she had been the victim of a nefarious plot. Hitler, feeling very embarrassed, promised to resolve the matter. That same evening, echoing his employee's arguments, he admitted to us that there was no proof his former cook's grandmother was Jewish, but that her name, which was of Turkish origin, had probably misled his staff. Unfortunately, the same staff did not allow themselves to be put off, and the poor woman was definitively banished from the stove, where the vegetarian meals of Germany's greatest hypocrite were simmering away sadly.

I would like to end this chapter by reporting the tribulations Hitler had with the family of his propaganda minister, Goebbels [Joseph Goebbels (1887–1945)].

In terms of passionate intelligence, Goebbels was undoubtedly superior to all those who made up Hitler's entourage. From the very beginning, Hitler valued him both as a genius propagandist and as a comrade in arms, and often referred to him as the conqueror of Berlin. He enjoyed the company of his club-footed minister, and every time Goebbels's Machiavellian face appeared, I sensed that Hitler felt genuine joy. Their conversations were always lively and peppered with witticisms, while Goebbels's brilliant intelligence and acerbic debates truly overwhelmed every guest at the dinner table. He possessed the tremendous gift of being able to ridicule a person by imitating their actions or by relating anecdotes about them, all told with a surprising verve and a dash of realism. Goebbels was a genius competitor and a formidable opponent who used the most devious methods to achieve what he wanted.

Hitler was a frequent visitor to the Goebbels house until 1939. He had a great affection for Frau Goebbels, who, despite her exuberant nature, could be very reserved and distant. Her wit and innate elegance exercised an indisputable charm over all who met her. Hitler adored the six Goebbels children, who were all remarkably well behaved and precociously intelligent, and his eyes would mist over whenever he spoke of them. Hitler also accepted Goebbels's invitations because it gave him the opportunity to meet artists, whom he always enjoyed being surrounded by.

It is worth noting that Goebbels had the rare privilege of being able to tell Hitler a political joke, often enjoying his wit more than the story itself. I often heard Hitler call Goebbels a '*durchtrieben Hund*' or '*schlauer Fuchs*',[1] etc., thus paying tribute to the intelligence and cunning of his propaganda minister.

Goebbels, who never practised austerity, was nevertheless not materialistic either. Only intelligence and wit had any certain value in his eyes. Although pretentious and full of himself, unlike Göring, whom he cordially detested, he practised moderation. In his role as minister of propaganda, he was able to dominate everyone thanks to various tricks he had perfected admirably, although the over-repeated use of these gradually diminished their effectiveness. Nevertheless, Goebbels was a fierce fighter who knew how to play to his strengths.

In 1940, the personal relationship between Goebbels and Hitler cooled noticeably. The minister of propaganda had put his position in jeopardy thanks to his innumerable liaisons, which had now become public knowledge. His relationship with the film actress Lída Baarová caused such a scandal that Frau Goebbels decided to divorce him, but Hitler opposed the breakup for reasons of domestic and foreign policy. The fate of the children was also very close to his heart. Goebbels and his wife were summoned to Berchtesgaden for reconciliation, promising Hitler that they would resume their life together. A photograph of the entire Goebbels family was taken for the occasion and distributed in the newspapers to put an end to the unpleasant rumours that had been circulating among the German population.

Hitler was particularly disappointed by the intransigent attitude shown by Frau Goebbels during the reconciliation talks. He accused her of dramatising the matter and, above all, of broadcasting private scenes and conversations that were none of the public's business. He was all the more disappointed by Frau Goebbels's obstinacy because at that time she had begun an affair with State Secretary Hanke [Karl Hanke (1903–45)]. Hitler never forgave Frau Goebbels for her careless behaviour and from that moment on treated her in such an impersonal and distant manner that she no longer stayed until the end of the parties at which they had the opportunity to meet.

However, I believe it was Eva Braun who was largely responsible for this strictness. Eva suffered from a painful inferiority complex in the presence of Frau Goebbels, who crushed her with her wit and charm, and her nasty remarks directed at Frau Goebbels obviously had an influence on Hitler.

He later confided to me that he sincerely regretted no longer being able to visit the Goebbels family home. He missed the pleasant society he had been accustomed to mixing with there, but the scandal had been pushed too far for him to turn back. Goebbels himself made only rare visits to headquarters, but with the increase in air raids on Berlin, during which Goebbels showed remarkable dedication in organising anti-aircraft defences and disaster relief, Hitler finally put the past behind him and called on Goebbels again.

By the end of the war, relations between Hitler and Frau Goebbels had returned to normal. He had forgiven her for her misconduct and the scandal it had caused to such an extent that he invited the whole family to take refuge in his personal bunker. Goebbels's suicide, which also involved the deaths of his wife and six children, was the logical culmination of a life entirely sacrificed to a propaganda ideal whose favourite weapons were slander and lies.

X

The leader of an army must live with the same simplicity as the men he commands.

Hitler

Hitler liked to surround himself with works of art, claiming that the decor had a calming effect on his frazzled nerves. When he stayed at the Berghof, I often saw him standing in deep contemplation in front of the paintings in the large, luxuriously decorated hall. With his eyes fixed on the painting, he would take a few steps forwards and backwards or move from side to side in order to capture the finest detail or take it in from a new angle. With his hand above his eyes to better focus his gaze, he would invite those near him to share his enthusiasm.

He often brought paintings down from one room or another on the first floor into the great hall, even moving paintings around himself to give them a different light. He would occupy himself like this for hours: it was his favourite pastime.

He enjoyed society, but in a lecturer's way. After his office work, he needed to relax. At first, he would still attend theatre performances from time to time and then go on to a brasserie, where he would spend a few hours among artists. The casual conversations he enjoyed there were an excellent tonic for him.

He would also sometimes visit friends and regularly called on the Goebbels and Ley families, where he again met famous artists.

Hitler hated bourgeois society and regularly refused invitations from senior army officers and noble families. He found the environment far too rigid and conventional for his dynamic nature, while also fearing the curiosity of such circles, where he often felt he was being observed like a museum piece. When he felt comfortable in society, however, he could be a very fine and eloquent conversationalist.

Yet this life changed completely from the first day of the war. Everything in the headquarters from where he directed operations was simple and austere. His adage was: 'Soldiers must know that their leader shares the same deprivations as they do.'

At the beginning of the Polish campaign, Hitler directed operations from a special train stationed in the vicinity of Gogolin. Every morning, he drove to the front line for inspections, before returning in the evenings, dusty and dirty. Before he left, he would always dictate calls and orders of the day to me, addressed to the soldiers. During the siege of Warsaw, he appealed to the population to leave the city. It was only towards the end of the campaign that he moved to the Sopot casino.

At the start of the French campaign, he had to make do with a regimental Command Post in the Eifel, comprising a very small bedroom and an office for himself, and a kitchen and some rooms for his adjutants and staff. A wooden hut was hastily erected in front of the bunker to serve as a dining room. All the furniture was made of white wood, with the seats, chairs and armchairs made of rattan. This was where Hitler took his meals, surrounded by his associates. He called this headquarters the 'Felsennest' (Rocky Eyrie), and everyone in his entourage who could not be accommodated in the shelter lived in the nearest village.

I will always remember the morning of 10 May 1940, when we arrived at the famous Rocky Eyrie. Hitler gathered his small General Staff and his associates around him and from the top of the bunker announced to us in a firm and declamatory voice that, that very morning, the French campaign had just been launched. All around us, banks of fog filled the Eifel valleys, as the first birds rose from the trees dripping with dew. From afar, the muffled rumbling of the guns reached us as a new page of history was beginning.

To our surprise, Hitler was very pleased with the rudimentary setup. He stayed outdoors as much as possible and I would see him pacing in front of the bunker, deep in thought.

As victories came one after another at a rapid pace, Hitler was always in a good mood. More than once in the following years, when a new sensational setback for the Wehrmacht was announced, he would speak bitterly about the famous Rocky Eyrie, where the situation had been completely different.

Hitler left the Eifel to follow the advance of our troops and settled in Brûly-de-Pesche, a small town located 100 kilometres [62 miles] from Brussels. Hitler occupied a wooden hut, while his staff was stationed in the rectory and the school. The nave of the small church, whose walls had been freshly whitewashed and whose choir was hidden by a large curtain, served as a dining room and cinema. A small air-raid shelter was hastily built next to the hut. Hitler never went there, but he followed the flights of the enemy squadrons that passed over us with interest. Once, incendiary bombs fell on the houses where his guard detachment and the Gestapo who were part of the retinue were quartered. Nevertheless, everyone continued to stand outside as the Allied planes flew over.

Hitler had named this headquarters 'Wolfsschlucht' [Wolf's Gorge], and it was there that he was told of France's surrender. In exuberant joy, Hitler slapped his thighs and did a little dance. Field Marshal Keitel then made a speech and invited all those present to drink to the health of the greatest conqueror of all time.

Hitler first wanted to revisit the bunker in France where he had spent a large part of the First World War, before heading to Paris, where he visited Les Invalides, the Opéra, etc. On his return, he proudly told us that he had found his way around the maze of corridors at the Opéra more easily than his guides. He had studied the construction of the Opera House as a teenager in Vienna, and all the architectural details were still etched in his memory.

Hitler did not leave his special train during the campaign in Yugoslavia as it allowed him to draw up plans for the Russian campaign in peace. When the blitzkrieg on the Russian colossus began, he was on the border of East Prussia, 14 kilometres [9 miles] from a sad provincial town called Rastenburg. This facility was given the name 'Wolfsschanze', and when I asked him why the name 'Wolf' came up so often in the designation of his headquarters, he explained that, in the underground, before the abortive Munich Putsch, he had been given the name Wolf.

There was enthusiasm among us all, but Hitler remained surprisingly serious. When his adjutant – who believed he knew Russia after a short stay there – confidently asserted that this campaign would be as short as the others and that this immense country would burst like a soap bubble, Hitler thoughtfully replied that he compared Russia to the famous ghost ship from the well-known Wagnerian opera instead. Then he added: 'At the start of each campaign, we push open a huge door that leads to a room plunged into darkness. You never know what lies behind it.'

However, he became more optimistic after the German troops enjoyed their initial successes. I remember in August 1941, while we were having tea at the casino, Hitler was staring at a huge map on the wall. His eyes had that mysterious sparkle of a soothsayer in a trance, which was customary for him in such circumstances, and in his rough bass voice he pronounced this prophecy: 'In a few weeks, we'll be in Moscow. There's no doubt about it. I will raze this damned city and build an artificial lake there that will supply power stations. The name of Moscow must disappear for ever.' We all felt a shiver run down our spines.

When, surprised by the rigours of a terrible winter, the German armies remained paralysed in the frozen expanses of a white Russia, although Hitler sometimes had fits of temper, he remained confident of an imminent victory: 'There's only a thin veil left to pierce. A little patience is needed. Russian resistance cannot last.'

However, our monotonous stay in the Wolfsschanze continued. During the summer of 1942, Hitler temporarily established himself in a new headquarters, called 'Werwolf', near Vinnytsia. There, at least, we lived in houses built from logs, which made the return to the bunkers of the Wolfsschanze in October that same year all the more painful.

As the Russian campaign progressed, with all its ups and downs, the Wolfsschanze was completed. Gradually a cinema, a teahouse and a very comfortable villa (for Göring) were built, even though Göring only made brief appearances there, twice a month. Hitler justified the construction of this sumptuous villa by philosophically admitting that there were people who, in order to wage war, felt the need to surround themselves with comfortable luxury.

From then on, life became more pleasant. A large café was built, where Hitler's entourage would hold parties, but while each of us was happy not to have to sleep in the bunker any more, Hitler stubbornly refused to leave his. We tried to explain to him that this termite lifestyle was unhygienic, but he claimed he could not sleep in the huts because they were too echoey and so he spent the last two years of the war buried in his shelter, emerging now and again only to breathe a few breaths of fresh air. While we had all suffered from circulation problems and headaches after sleeping in the confined air of the bunkers, he seemed to feel particularly comfortable in such an artificial atmosphere.

The rooms he occupied were furnished with rudimentary simplicity. In peacetime, Hitler would spend vast sums on decorating his apartments with flowers, but now he did not even want the wildflower bouquets with which we adorned our offices.

'My main concern', he declared, 'is that this headquarters should have none of the luxury and comfort that the soldier is deprived of. I've often found that when my officers and soldiers come here to receive their medals, the simplicity that surrounds me impresses them favourably.'

The disaster at Stalingrad plunged Hitler into deep depression. He was obsessed with Paulus's [Friedrich Wilhelm Ernst Paulus (1890–1957)] surrender and so to distract him, Bormann decided to give him a new sheepdog as a present. However, Hitler increasingly avoided society and became downright misogynistic. He no longer took meals with his staff in the officers' mess after General Jodl [Alfred Jodl (1890–1946)] hurt him terribly by publicly daring to contradict him at the table. From then on, he buried himself completely in his bunker, taking his meals alone, one-on-one with his German Shepherd. His great distraction was feeding the animal, while he himself, between his four concrete walls, swallowed his vegetarian meals with sadness.

This crisis of depression lasted for several months until, finally, the monastic solitude started to weigh on him, and he began to invite various officers from his General Staff who had come from Berlin to share his modest repast with him. However, his guests could only talk to him about work matters, which displeased him, so he changed his mind once again and from then on ate his meals in the presence of one of my colleagues and me. We were strictly forbidden to talk about work or even to allude to the war. While the Wehrmacht was being bled white by the furious assaults of the Russian armies thousands of kilometres away, Hitler would hold forth interminably on art and literature.

In the morning, Hitler would take a walk with Blondi, his German Shepherd. He had built a track strewn with obstacles that he made her jump over; it was the only pleasure and distraction he allowed himself. He never attended film screenings, except for the news, but only to see the work of the censors.

Before the retreat from Stalingrad, Hitler would still organise musical evenings from time to time. Motionless in an armchair, he took immense pleasure in listening to Beethoven symphonies, Wagner operas or Hugo Wolf's *Lieder* for hours on end. Later, he would come to hate these performances, so we would spend all our evenings with him, listening to him talk. But just as the records he used to play were nothing more than an eternal repetition of the same works, his subjects of conversation likewise hardly varied. More than ever, he loved to tell us stories of his youth, describing his difficult adolescence in Vienna and evoking the period of struggle which preceded his seizure of power. Even the greater subjects, such as the question of the origins of man, had been repeated so much that we knew them by heart. We were tired of such refrains! World events and news from the front were systematically ignored. The war was never mentioned.

When it came to talking about our life at the Wolfsschanze, the conversation invariably turned to the antics or disobedience of Blondi, his dog, or even the exploits of a cat that I had introduced into the bunker in violation of the regulations. Hitler hated cats because they hunted birds, but gradually, however, he grew accustomed to the creature.

Hitler was possessed by jealousy and envy, becoming furious whenever he saw Peter, the cat, and Blondi show affection to someone other than him. When his dog went up to someone confidently, he immediately suspected the person in question of having enticed her with a piece of meat, something that was strictly forbidden. However, his vanity soon took over and he always ended up declaring that it was a waste of time trying to gain Blondi's affection, since the dog only loved her master.

By the end of 1944, the situation at the Wolfsschanze was becoming increasingly worrying. Enemy squadrons flew over us every day, and Hitler kept predicting a surprise attack as a warning to the unwary among us who never took cover. On the other hand, he persisted in remaining in such an advanced position, even though he was being urged from all sides to return to Berlin. Invariably, he would reply: 'It's my duty to remain here. This will reassure the population, and my soldiers would never allow the front to withdraw to where their Führer has his headquarters. It will encourage them to fight with greater ardour.'

Hitler occupied another bunker during his long illness, so we took the opportunity to reinforce the first one by increasing the thickness of the ceiling to 5 metres of concrete. The labourers worked there until the day before the headquarters were evacuated under Russian pressure. On the very day of departure, all the facilities were destroyed. The same thing happened in Berlin; when the Russian troops reached the city gates, the famous bunker in the Chancellery was still being reinforced.

From mid-December 1944 until the end of January 1945, Hitler stayed in his first headquarters, the 'Adlerhorst' [Eagle's Nest], near Bad Nauheim. Due to the constant air attacks to which the capital was subjected, when he went to Berlin, he set up his bedroom in the Chancellery bunker. Meetings with his associates were held in the large hall of the Chancellery and he took his meals with us in the small corner room. However, as meetings and meals were constantly being interrupted by alerts, Hitler one day decided he would no longer leave his shelter. He lived in a very narrow room with space only for a small desk, an uncomfortable sofa, a table and three armchairs. It was cold and unpleasant. On the left was the bathroom and on the right the bedroom, which was also reduced to the dimensions of a prison cell.

The desk was completely dwarfed by a painting of Frederick the Great. You always had the impression that old 'Fritz' was judging you harshly with his intense gaze. The narrowness of the room – I had to move the chairs every time to let someone pass – and its atmosphere quite literally paralysed my reflexes and thoughts.

At around 6 o'clock in the morning, when he received us in the room after the night meeting, Hitler was far from capable of bringing a breath of fresh air into this grave-like atmosphere. He would lie on the small sofa, completely exhausted by the endless discussions he had had with his military advisers. His physical and intellectual decline progressed day by day, despite his desperate efforts to combat it. Yet when we entered the room, he still found the strength to stand up to greet us. He then stood before us, arm and leg trembling, before sinking back onto the sofa as his valet placed his feet on a large cushion. I could read only one wish in his apathetic gaze: to finally be able to satisfy his hunger with cocoa and cakes. His greed for pastries had become unhealthy, and whereas before he never took more than three portions, he now needed a plate full to the brim. I no longer understood how he, who continued to advocate a Spartan life, could stuff himself with sweets and cakes for pleasure. He explained to us that he ate less at dinner so that he could eat more pastries. He did not speak as he indulged in his favourite satisfaction, swallowing the pastry greedily, as if he were afraid it might be taken away from him. As an excuse, he told us that he had never been able to understand why a man did not like sweets.

Gorging himself on these incredible delicacies, at a time when Berlin was turning into a bonfire, alarmed me, and I felt as if I was living a nightmare in the presence of this human ruin. Hitler's very appearance had become distressing. His faded skin, cloudy eyes, thin, slightly blue lips with crumbs stuck to them, inspired both disgust and pity in me.

But even better: Hitler, the sworn enemy of alcohol, was now encouraging us to drink. However, it was true that without waiting for his agreement, those around him indulged in alcohol with frenzy, trying to forget the abnormal existence we led in that concrete vault.

Those morning teas lasted for two hours. With his shuffling step, Hitler would then go to Blondi's bed and begin to stroke her at length. She had had puppies in March and Hitler had chosen one of them to raise by himself, without any help. He would take the young dog on his knees and stroke him, constantly calling his name, 'Wolfi', in an infinitely gentle voice. Then he would bring the young animal back to its mother and finally take his leave. By then it was 8 o'clock. He had little time to sleep. The sirens sounded regularly around 11. Hitler never lay down during the air raids on Berlin and was worried that a bomb would hit the bunker at an angle, tearing off a section of the side wall. As the entire building was surrounded by a sheet of water, he feared drowning in the shelter. Therefore, as soon as enemy bombers approached, he would get up, get dressed and even take care to shave. He never stayed alone in his apartment and instead would come to join us in the small hall.

Hitler liked to linger over dinner, which usually took place around 9 or 10 o'clock. Throughout the meal, our radio reproduced the monotonous call of the special police transmitter. During a raid, Hitler would be completely focused on the news from the station about the progress of the attack. We would be at his side, unmoving, watching for the explosions from which the Chancellery quarters were never exempt. The day after the attack on 3 February 1945, for example, fifty-eight high-explosive bombs fell in our vicinity, and every time one of the devices crashed near the bunker, the whole thing would shake. It felt as if it was literally swinging, and when the electric light flickered due to the shaking of the building, Hitler's voice rose as if in a dream: 'The bomb could've hit us that time.' His face was livid, his features tense, and his gaze wandered anxiously from one of us to another. Clearly, Hitler was afraid.

After the attacks, he asked for reports on the damage caused. He read them silently, never making any comments. Then he would retire to his bedroom to read a paper or rest a little, in order to be ready for the next night conference. This last meeting always began after midnight and often lasted until dawn, then it was the usual tea, petting the dogs, followed by a little sleep until the next alert, which always lasted until lunch. Hitler then called the afternoon meeting, and the same obsessive repetitions began all over again.

Our life, punctuated by air raids, meetings and meals, all in constant contact with the fallen potentate, passed in a hallucinatory monotony, far from the reality in which Germany was dissolving.

XI

The tragedy of this war is that three men of genius are fighting each other.
Hitler (during an evening of depression)

One of Hitler's greatest weaknesses was his almost complete ignorance of the mindset and actions of foreign countries. He had hardly ever left the borders of Greater Germany and had deeply mistaken ideas about foreigners. All his knowledge in the fields of geography, economics and history had been borrowed from literature or drawn from his ambassadors' reports. Over the years, as he lived more and more isolated from the real world and the reports from his observers abroad only reached him after being rigorously filtered by his advisers, he formed an increasingly distorted picture of what was happening beyond Germany.

No ministry made as many mistakes as the Ministry of Foreign Affairs did. It was there the most insane ideas were welcomed, particularly those relating to the famous EUR-ASIA project. Nowhere else was the soul of the people been trampled upon with such blind ignorance, and yet Hitler approved of it. The geo-economic reshaping of the world, in the levelling of so-called 'inferior' countries and races, provided material for his most audacious and chimerical fantasies, and it was in this field that his divinatory predictions developed with the exuberance of an exotic flower.

Ribbentrop [Joachim von Ribbentrop (1893–1946)] – the minister representing wines – was one of the people Hitler liked to make fun of. His criticisms should not be taken too seriously, however, because whenever someone dared to attack Ribbentrop, Hitler always took the minister's side, even going so far as to regard Ribbentrop as the greatest German foreign minister since Bismarck [Otto von Bismarck (1815–1898)].

Laughing, he once told me how he had tried to introduce Ribbentrop to Hindenburg [Paul von Hindenburg (1847–1934)] in 1932, during his negotiations with the latter for the seizure of power. In his deep bass voice, the senile field marshal had refused to meet him, replying imperturbably: 'Leave me alone with this champagne merchant.'

Ribbentrop was the most paper-happy of all the ministers in the Third Reich, although Hitler paid no attention to the endless memoranda submitted to him. I often saw him throw them back on his desk in a fit of temper, declaring that he had no intention of involving himself in the intrigues between the various ministers. Those representing foreign affairs and propaganda were constantly engaged in a merciless struggle, and the question of which of the two had the right to control the press was never definitively decided by Hitler.

Yet it is not surprising that Hitler was entirely inspired by Ribbentrop in all matters relating to England and considered him to be the top specialist in English affairs. It was Ribbentrop who constantly stirred up the Führer's hatred of Albion. I do not exaggerate when I say he was exclusively responsible for Hitler's refusal to accept a final attempt at negotiations with the British ambassador in Berlin on the fate of the Danzig corridor, on the eve of our troops' entry into Poland.

It was also through Ribbentrop's influence that Hitler became dominated by a morbid aversion to everything English towards the end of the war. However, as late as 1940, when Italy signed the famous Pact of Steel with Germany, Hitler made the following remark to me: 'I would have preferred to sign an alliance with the English. They are racially much closer to the Germans than the Latins.'

Although I was unable to verify it, Hitler claimed to be able to follow a conversation in English and French, provided the flow was not particularly fast. He also told me: 'I never make an effort to speak in a foreign language because the time my interpreters spend translating questions and answers is too precious to me in a diplomatic negotiation. The downtime allows me to think and find concise and striking formulas for my answers.'

As early as 1925, Hitler had begun to write a secret book on foreign policy. No one knew about the pile of papers covered in his small, tight, almost illegible handwriting. Very rarely, and only when he was consumed with worry, did he allude to the composition he was working on. Shortly after war was declared in 1939, while in a fit of megalomania, he announced to Hess: 'Now all my work is falling apart. My book was written for nothing.'

I believe Hess was the only one aware of the personal ideas

Hitler had developed in this manuscript, and therefore the explanation for his later escapade to England could be found in its pages.

At the end of 1944, Hitler informed me of his intention to give me a very long dictation and asked me to be ready over the following days. He never carried out his plan, although I am convinced that he had intended to dictate his political testimony to me.

Before the war he had declared to me, and I believe that this idea truly corresponded to his views, that for him, an alliance with England represented the ideal solution to the problem of global domination. He believed the English navy and the German land army were powerful enough to rebuild the world on new foundations.

Hitler was a great admirer of England's colonial policy, and I know that in 1926 he expressed the following to his closest associates: 'I hope the crown of the British Empire will not lose any of its pearls; that would be a catastrophe for humanity.'

In the years before the war, when German public opinion expressed its sympathy for the independence movement in India, he declared: 'I forbid my people to be seduced by this general craze for Gandhi. Freedom is not won with looms, but with cannons.'

On the other hand, Hitler showed unreserved admiration for Japan. The heads of the Wehrmacht's General Staff, who were always opposed to a policy of rapprochement with this country, only saw Germany's salvation in a close alliance with Russia. But Hitler was not to be persuaded. This was one of the reasons for his disagreement with von Blomberg, who then had to disappear because, among other differences, he had systematically opposed Hitler's favourite idea of an alliance with Japan.

Hitler was well aware of the enormity of his pro-Japanese policy from a racial point of view. He once told me: 'I'm accused of making a deal with the Japanese. What does that mean? It's true that they are different from us; they have yellow skin and slanted eyes, but, importantly, they are fighting against the Americans. This is the only reason why they're useful to us and why I consider them to be allies.'

He delved even further into his mental reserves in the face of the Japanese problem. When Singapore was taken by Mikado's troops, Ribbentrop wanted to celebrate the occasion with major events in the German press and radio, but when he submitted his project to Hitler, the latter did not agree and told him: 'I don't know, my dear Ribbentrop, whether your plans are wise. In the face of history, we must think in centuries, and sooner or later, the great explanation between the white race and the yellow race will come.'

In his public speeches, his judgements on the foreign statesmen he was at war with were filled with hatred and disdain, although it should not be forgotten that such assessments were mainly intended for domestic propaganda in Germany. Conversely, Hitler spoke in a much more levelled manner about foreign heads of state when discussing international problems within his small circle, and broadly speaking, as I can deduce from his numerous conversations, these were his real opinions.

Roosevelt. Hitler never concealed his dislike for the president of the United States. He called him a public charlatan and claimed that he had launched his country into war for the sole purpose of covering up the failure of his domestic policy from the world. Deep down, however, he saw in Roosevelt a statesman of a higher calibre than his own, and there was a feeling of envy and hateful impotence in the very violence of the epithets he used against him. Hitler was a master at leading the masses but had a vague feeling that in this area he was no match for the 'chess player' Roosevelt. Subconsciously, he admired the political moves the president had made, which had resulted in the United States accepting the idea of going to war. This is where we must look for the real reason for the irascibility Hitler displayed whenever Roosevelt's name was mentioned.

Stalin. Hitler never tried to hide the esteem and admiration he felt for the leader of the USSR. He was the only foreign statesman he would have liked to have known better. Whenever one of his envoys returned from a trip to Russia, he would make them tell him their impressions in minute detail and, very often, could afterwards not help exclaiming, in a fit of enthusiasm: 'This Stalin is a dirty beast, but, really, we must recognise that he is an extraordinary man' (*Ein Biest, aber ein ganzer Kerl*).

Churchill. Hitler showed complete contempt for the English prime minister and did this not only in his public speeches, but even in conversations with his close friends. He did not grant Churchill the slightest of favours and instead conferred on him complete and total condemnation. When Churchill's name was mentioned, Hitler did not even concede a semblance of admiration for the courage with which the latter had continued an almost hopeless struggle, by putting the whole weight of his personality into the endeavour. The contempt he heaped on Churchill came up again and again in the fireside chats. Curiously, however, Hitler did not manifest this in an outburst of anger, as he always did with Roosevelt. Taking into account his unfathomable complex, perhaps we should interpret Hitler's attitude as an unacknowledged recognition of the merits of the man who had defied everything alone following the French campaign.

The sincere admiration Hitler had always felt for English colonial policy ceased to manifest itself in the later years. During the war, Hitler saw Churchill as nothing more than a helpless tool in the hands of Roosevelt and Stalin, and the gravedigger of the British Empire.

*

Hitler showed a deep and sincere friendship for Mussolini, almost until the end. He felt linked to the Duce by the paths they had taken. However, he noted with regret that Mussolini did not enjoy the same absolute freedom of action as he did, instead finding himself dependent on the Royal House of Italy. He never stopped reproaching him for it. After his official visit to Rome in 1937, he told me that he had been appalled to see the Duce treated with such haughty condescension by King Victor Emmanuel. He confessed to me that he had had to force himself not to interrupt his trip in protest at the constant humiliations to which Mussolini had been subjected. At the military parade in Rome, seats were set up for the royals and himself, while Mussolini had to stand behind them for the entire parade! 'It disgusted me to such an extent that I almost made an official scene. It was only out of respect for the Duce that I didn't give free rein to my annoyance, faced with such a lack of tact and respect.'

After the betrayal and collapse of Italy, Hitler's genuine sympathy for the Duce was barely veiled, and I believe it was tinged with a feeling of compassion and pity. He treated Mussolini like a younger brother who could make up for a youthful mistake by following his elder brother's instructions to the letter. Hitler stubbornly refused to follow Mussolini in his efforts to convince him that international events now dictated a reversal of policy in the face of various problems.

Hitler's great disappointment only manifested itself after Skorzeny [Otto Skorzeny (1908–1975)] freed the Duce. Mussolini's 'diary', which was found during the raid and which Hitler personally read, shed new light on the founder of fascism's character. Hitler gave us some of the details during his talks, emphasising the weaknesses and changing duplicity of the 'lion of the peninsula'. With dismay, he summed up his painful surprise in these words: 'I admit I was wrong. Mussolini was small minded. Now I have irrefutable proof of this.'

XII

Your best ally during the war was Hitler himself.
Göring (during his interrogation in May 1945)

This statement by the former Reichsmarschall, made during the initial days of his captivity, shows the constant tension that existed between Hitler and the Wehrmacht leaders. These continuing and tragic disagreements had arisen when, shortly after taking power, the Wehrmacht realised that the National Socialist state had taken root among the proletarian masses instead of in the core of the intellectual classes.

It should be added that Hitler coped very easily without 'intellectuals' during his period of struggle. Very often, he even rejected their offer of collaboration as he fiercely pursued his goal to build the Party with the working class as its sole base.

In the years that followed, the power and influence of the 'Gauleiters' and other important officials only grew. The first people to join the Hitler movement enjoyed a prestige that was often incomprehensible. While officers, old civil servants or scientists often lost their positions due to their desire for independence, the 'old hands' of the Party remained firmly attached to the regime, even when they had committed very serious errors.

This state of affairs caused painful disappointment among the officers of a certain age, and very quickly this resentment led them to distance themselves increasingly from Hitler. The latter had no excuses and could no longer even claim that the Party was still suffering from the diseases of adaptation that strike every revolutionary movement. For his part, Hitler increasingly distanced himself from his General Staff, which had at first enjoyed his full confidence. There is no doubt that this change of attitude was due in part to machinations of Party powerbrokers who feared rivalry from the army, which they saw as a reactionary clique. Such insinuations found fertile ground in Hitler's innate distrust.

There were several points of friction. The Wehrmacht generals, particularly the older ones, spoke out strongly against Hitler's haste to overturn the organisation of the army in order to adapt it to his new policies. However, Hitler saw this advice of caution as cowardice and lacking in decisiveness. Field Marshals von Blomberg and von Fritsch [Werner von Fritsch (1880–1939)] were the first victims.

Until the outbreak of war, Hitler had given the generals complete freedom when it came to the training of troops; he was more interested in the development of various weapons. I will only cite one small example that I experienced personally.

In 1936 we were sitting with him at a café terrace in Munich when a newspaper vendor offered us some illustrated magazines. On one of the first pages were pictures of 200 Russian paratroopers falling from the sky in a collective drop. We burst out laughing, thinking that this was a huge error as the men would just be targets for a magnificent pigeon shoot. Only Hitler remained serious. He asked for some scissors, cut out the photograph and, without saying a word, put it in his pocket. I know that he called Göring two days later and gave him a draft regulation for the formation of the first German parachute regiment.

After Hitler's first successes in Poland and then Norway, his faith in his infallibility only grew. He became incredibly touchy when someone dared to disagree with him and reacted brutally against such an 'insult to his genius'.

However, when he wanted to launch a general offensive against France in the winter of 1939–40, he once again encountered opposing opinions from the Wehrmacht leaders. It was explained to him that the difficult terrain of the Eifel and the Ardennes practically excluded a winter campaign, never mind that the bulk of the German troops were not yet sufficiently trained to fight anyway. Once again, Hitler called such reservations cowardice and, following this incident (November 1939), made a sensational speech.

Göring knew his master better than anyone else and never confronted him head on. He also thought that the winter campaign would be disastrous but, clever as he was, refrained from making his opinion known. Instead, he waited quietly until the day before the general attack was due to take place before declaring to Hitler that the Luftwaffe was not in a position to take part in the operations due to the poor weather conditions. He repeated this little game three times. Finally, the offensive was resumed.

Hitler, though, had luck smiling down on him. It was he who had decided to push through the Ardennes to break the barrier around which the French armies of the north and east were pivoting, and, against all odds, events proved him right. The success certainly intoxicated him and from that date on, he directed all operations himself and no longer accepted any contradiction to his orders.

At the same time, his distrust of most of the Wehrmacht's leaders only grew, even reaching the point of obsession. One evening, I heard the following words from his lips: 'The Grand General Staff of the German Army is the last of the masonic lodges that unfortunately I forgot to dissolve.'

However, he was furious that he could not do without the knowhow of these same officers, and therefore persisted, as far as possible, in minimising their worth. The glory of his generals made him green with envy. When a famous military writer one day dared to claim in the press that the Führer was lucky to be surrounded by such a competent General Staff, the statement was interpreted as an insult and the imprudent author was banned from any future literary activity.

As well as lacking confidence in his General Staff, Hitler's distrust meant it also led him to intervene at lower levels. He took away virtually all initiative from the commanders of large units and when he submitted operational plans to his colleagues, he not only provided the outlines, but worked out its execution down to the smallest detail. Only his plans were to be transmitted, in the form of orders, to the various army groups. It goes without saying that this continual interference in all phases of operations meant that mentally, Hitler was catastrophically overworked. The disasters that followed the first successes of the campaigns in the East also revealed how catastrophic this method was for the Wehrmacht.

It was in his dealings with his army leaders and in the implacable manner in which he broke and punished them that his unnatural character manifested itself so freely. There is no example in history of such a 'waltz' of marshals!

It should be noted, though, that for certain strategic problems, Hitler had the astonishing ability to see clearly and correctly. He often found happy solutions to difficulties previously considered practically insurmountable, and he did this simply by letting his common sense speak. This exceptional gift of reducing the most complex problems down to their simplest expression cannot be disputed. Thanks to his phenomenal memory, he had acquired a respectable stock of military knowledge. He had enthusiastically read all the global studies on motorised warfare and rightly considered himself the spiritual father of 'armoured vehicles' in the context of large strategic manoeuvres.

However, he had absolutely no experience in the practical conduct of operations, and his stubbornness in constantly interfering in the execution of his own plans led to disaster for the Wehrmacht. The example of Stalingrad clearly shows the harmful consequences of his obstinacy. Whenever it was suggested to him that he should order the Sixth Army to withdraw, he would proudly reply: 'I know the Sixth Amy and its valiant commander. The fortress of Stalingrad will hold thanks to the help I'm sending.'

The Sixth Army was ordered to resist at all costs, but in the meantime clung on to just a few ruins of the city before being swallowed up in the snowy steppes, under the relentless attacks of the Russian troops. Field Marshal Paulus had issued a dramatic appeal in which he explained that aerial resupply of his surrounded army was impossible and that all attempts by other German armies to approach had been repulsed. Yet Hitler stuck to his decision. He did not want to admit that fate had turned against him and that he was going to experience defeat after a period of continuous victories.

This brutal obstinacy was evident in all his orders issued to the troops. In 1944, we know the implacable cruelty with which he threatened to shoot any soldier who deserted a position under pressure from the enemy: 'Every city, every village must be defended like a fortress, right down to the last cartridge. Not a single piece of land must be abandoned to the enemy.'

This order had dire consequences for troop morale during the Allied invasion of Europe. Towards the end, Hitler needed someone to blame for every defeat and every retreat. As setbacks continued to befall him, the 'consumption' of commanders in large units became frightening, and it has been calculated that in February 1945, an army commander would last no more than a month in charge.

These measures were disastrous for the stability of the conduct of the war. The troops no longer understood what was happening, and confidence in their leaders suffered as a result. Every time Hitler dismissed one of his field marshals, he did so in a violent fit of anger. Indeed, his hysterical outburst overawed them so much that they could hardly find the arguments necessary to justify themselves. These men, who had just escaped the fantastical sufferings of the Russian front, who had become accustomed to measuring themselves against death on the frozen plains, were literally frightened by the raging ferocity of their Führer.

After the assassination attempt of 20 July 1944, Hitler's hostility toward his General Staff increased even more. He was not at all surprised that the perpetrators who had tried to end his life had come from this milieu and saw this as proof that his distrust of his generals was fully justified. I remember that one day, when his German Shepherd disobeyed him, he scolded her by saying: 'Look me in the eyes, Blondi! Would you be as traitorous as the generals of my General Staff?'

Hitler saw the constant growth of SS units as a political asset in his fight against the General Staff and continually encouraged Himmler to take the best of the young recruits to form new SS divisions. Here, too, phenomenal mistakes were made. Himmler and Hitler's idea that racial purity and political training were more important to soldiers than proper training and education was simply shocking. And when Hitler went so far as to entrust the SS chief with the entire supplementary army and the Volksgrenadiere divisions, and even raised him to the command of an army group, there was no longer any doubt that he had definitively broken with the traditional and military principles which had made Germany great.

Yet even within the ranks of the SS, unexpected defections were to occur. The archetypical leader in SS combat units was undoubtedly Sepp Dietrich [(1892–1966)], who had risen from being a butcher's boy to the rank of Army Commanding General.

Sepp Dietrich. Hitler considered Sepp Dietrich to be a typical Landsknecht, hiding an ardent and proud soul beneath a brusque and sometimes clumsy exterior. He appreciated the simplicity of dress and spirit that Dietrich had retained, despite his glittering rise through the ranks of the black militia. The Führer was well aware that the SS held him in great esteem and sincerely venerated the one they informally called their 'Old Man'.

However, towards the end of the war, Machiavellian intrigues got the better of the unlimited trust that Hitler had placed in Sepp Dietrich for more than twenty years. I believe it was Fegelein, Eva Braun's brother-in-law, who did a great deal to sow suspicion in Hitler's heart towards Sepp Dietrich.

After the setbacks suffered by the 5th SS Panzer Army under Dietrich's command, particularly the resounding defeat in Austria on the way to the invading Russian army, Hitler had lost all confidence in his protégé. In his fury during those final days, he even forbade the SS units that made up the 5th SS Panzer Army from wearing their special armbands. Shortly afterwards, in a moment of melancholic depression, Hitler indulged in this uncompromising condemnation of Sepp Dietrich: 'Now even one of my SS generals has gone over to the ranks of the traitors.'

Towards the end, Hitler had only one aim: to gain time. During meetings with his associates, he spoke only about topics he found interesting and rarely let others speak. He had completely lost his sense of reality. He lived in a nebulous world, chasing dreams and chimeras. He still believed in victory with the obstinacy of a sick person who tries to convince themself that they will get better by tirelessly repeating that they will do so.

However, Hitler retained this exceptional gift, which he used to maintain his hold on the hesitant, affirming his faith in the final victory with such assurance that those around him continued to believe in the miracle. He constantly spoke of new weapons that would drive the invaders from the continent, promising that after this terrible war, Germany would be rebuilt more beautiful than before.

I believe he was truly convinced that weapons with terrible consequences would emerge from German laboratories and workshops in time to determine the outcome of the war. He shared his horrific visions with us. It is true that he had been planning this horrible end for a long time. I remember that in 1943 he had already pronounced the prophetic words: 'May God forgive me the last fifteen days of this war, because they'll be horrifying!'

However, he had to buy time while waiting for these apocalyptic measures. For Hitler, this meant declaring total war and launching poorly equipped territorials against enemy tanks. To slow the advance of the invaders, he organised a 'guerilla group', without realising that a partisan war was difficult to carry out bearing in mind Germany's geography. The trivial activities of the 'Werwolf'[1] has proven this. I have heard from witnesses, whose good faith I have no reason to suspect, that Hitler toyed with the idea of executing a certain number of Allied prisoners. This measure would have provoked reprisals and, in Hitler's mind, would have put an end to the increasing desertions from the ranks of the Wehrmacht.

Hitler justified these tyrannical measures by tirelessly repeating this proverb: 'A dead man can no longer defend himself.'

As long as there was a semblance of hope, Hitler fought back. He continued to resist, sending the very flower of German youth to be massacred. He did all this without thinking that he was dragging down an entire people with him, to whom he had promised a thousand-year era of bliss.

XIII

All that remains after a man dies are his works and the legacy he leaves behind.

Hitler

Hitler used to toss a coin when he did not want to appear to be imposing his will on people he wanted to protect, or when he himself was undecided on a secondary issue.

This gesture, which may be surprising, does not in any way prove that he was a gambler by nature. In the pre-war period, for example, when Hitler and some of the regulars in his entourage could not make up their minds as to whether they went for a drive or went to the mountains, he used to take a coin and toss it in the air; the side it landed on would then decide where they went. It was always the eagle side of the coin that was interpreted as representing the 'affirmative', and these decisions of fate were not to be argued against by anyone.

During the war, I no longer saw Hitler operate in this way, even for trivial decisions.

There were also rumours that the Führer let himself be advised by astrologers on the eve of important actions. I confess that there was never any question of such practices during our interviews, nor did I notice the slightest indication of them. He always vehemently rejected the idea that a man's fate depended on the star or constellation under which he was born and refuted this thesis by demonstrating that people born on the same day, in the same place and at the same time did not share identical destinies. He saw the clearest evidence of this in the case of twins. It is true that in his early days as a public agitator, when he was still very far from power, he had been greatly impressed by the predictions of a fortune-teller from Munich. However, although it seems that the future she predicted for him came true bit by bit, Hitler merely spoke of this coincidence ironically and considered it a joke. I have often heard it said that these professional charlatans should be banned from practising their mystifications. He also rejected the idea that certain days of the week, or certain numbers, could have an influence on our actions. When making an important decision, Hitler used to weigh it up carefully and calculate all the factors involved. Then, in determining when the decision should be translated into action, he let himself be guided almost entirely by intuition. I believe that Hitler – whom I had the opportunity to observe closely for many years – was 80 per cent cold and calculating, and that the rest of him was just intuition.

Just as Hitler exuded a magnetic power that affected those he interacted with, so his subconscious was subject to the powerful impulses of his intuitive mind. Very often, when he had predicted something against everyone's advice and then, to everyone's astonishment, the incredible had happened, he would say, laughingly: 'You see, once again, I had a good nose!'

These hunches, these inner warnings, played a very particular role in the attacks directed against him. To better understand their scope, it is worthwhile returning to the main assassination attempts where he was the target.

Before the assassination attempt at the Bürgerbräukeller in Munich on 9 November 1939 [*TN*: the date of the assassination attempt was 8 November 1939], Hitler had never considered the possibility of such an eventuality. Yet after this date, it was commonplace in conversations. In total, Hitler listed seven assassination attempts against his person, including Röhm's intention to oust him. According to Hitler, the leader of the SA was an anarchist who wanted to seize power at any cost and by any means. Röhm, a Landsknecht by nature, was not at all inspired by the Nazi ideal and the idea of creating a new order. Instead, his sole aim was to seize command of the Wehrmacht. Röhm intended to remove abruptly from command not only Field Marshal von Blomberg and a few other generals, but would not have hesitated, if necessary, to attack Hitler himself.

Blomberg's intelligence service had informed him of Röhm's intentions, and he had then warned Hitler that the Wehrmacht would revolt at such a change in command. Tensions between the Party and the army were becoming extreme, threatening Germany with a civil war.

When Hitler had indisputable evidence of his deputy's criminal plans, he acted with brutal speed to avert the danger. He confided to me that he had proof Röhm had also conspired with those abroad, and that General von Schleicher [Kurt von Schleicher (1882–1934)] was merely putty in his hands. 'It was thanks to my swift and ruthless actions that I prevented a misfortune far greater than the disappearance of that handful of men whom any High Court in Germany would have had the duty to condemn as traitors to their country.'

Hitler often jokingly remarked that his star had not always been as favourable to him as it had been in Röhm's case, where he had been warned in advance of the actions planned against him.

He told us that before he came to power, a man had tried to shoot him with a revolver in the hall of the Kaiserhof, while he was having tea there. Another time, sandwiches that had been prepared for him at the same hotel for a trip were poisoned. Hitler told us:

'Luckily, I wasn't hungry that day. I passed the sandwiches to my driver, Schreck, who immediately had a violent stomach pain and all the symptoms of poisoning. He was only saved by drastic intervention. With my delicate stomach, these little buns, buttered with cyanide, would certainly have caused me to pass from life to death. Brave Schreck, who was of a particularly robust constitution, was fortunate enough to escape.'

Another time, during a public meeting, Hitler noticed that a man sitting opposite him on the podium was extremely agitated. His behaviour seemed so bizarre to Hitler that he sensed danger and had the individual searched immediately. It was discovered that the man was carrying a bomb which, had it exploded, could have brought down the entire room.

In the winter of 1941–2, another attacker was exposed by Hitler thanks to their strange behaviour. He was a Swiss man whom Hitler had noticed every time he came down from the Berghof in Berchtesgaden. Suspecting something was wrong, Hitler rushed towards the man to question him. Rather disconcerted by this unexpected action, the man stammered out some excuses and claimed that he wanted to deliver a personal letter to Hitler. Hitler snatched the envelope from him and saw that it contained nothing but a blank sheet of paper. The man then confessed directly to Hitler that he had been lying in wait for him for weeks with the intention of shooting him dead.

Every time the Führer told us about the attacks in which he had nearly been the victim, he acknowledged that he had been helped by an unusual stroke of luck. However, he also stressed that his extraordinary flair had helped him a great deal to ward off these mortal dangers.

In the attack at the Bürgerbräukeller in Munich, the conspirators had prepared their assault with fiendish skill. The bomb was placed in such a way that Hitler would inevitably have been crushed under the ceiling, collapsing as it did at the exact spot where Hitler had been moments before. Once again, his divine intuition had saved him. While in previous years he had been in the habit of shaking hands individually with each of his former comrades in arms, this time, on the night of the assassination attempt, Hitler did not make this gesture of camaraderie. He explained to me later:

'I suddenly felt an urgent need to cut the meeting short so that I could return to Berlin that evening. In truth, there was no compelling reason for this, since there was nothing important wating for me in the capital; I just listened to this inner voice that was to save me. If I had, as usual, greeted my companions, as I intended to do at the beginning, my enemies would undoubtedly have succeeded in eliminating me. The explosion happened a quarter of an hour after I left.'

I found myself with Hitler on the train back to Berlin on the evening in question. He was witty and very animated, as he usually was after a successful meeting. Goebbels was also there and enlivened the conversation with his caustic wit. At that time, Hitler's entourage was still allowed to consume alcohol, so the entire special train was bathed in an atmosphere of infectious cheerfulness. The train stopped in Nuremberg for a short while, and it was Goebbels's job to gather news and send any urgent messages. When he returned to Hitler's saloon car, he told him what had happened after he had left Munich. Hitler, incredulous, did not comprehend it at first, but finally took the matter seriously after he saw little Goebbels's defeated expression. When there was no longer any doubt about the authenticity of the news, Hitler's face froze in a determined, hard mask. In his gaze, the mystical flame I knew he had during moments of great decision-making began to dance. In a voice sharp and hoarse with emotion, he exclaimed: 'Now I'm completely at peace; the fact that I left the Bürgerbräu earlier than usual is confirmation that Providence wants my destiny to be fulfilled.'

We were all glued to our seats with emotion, his words acting on us like the apotheosis of a drama with hallucinatory twists and turns.

But Hitler quickly came to his senses and took action. He asked for news of the wounded and instructed Schaub, his adjutant, to take care of the victims. Hitler then began to speculate about the possible origins of the conspirators. Schaub, who had already been drinking heavily, incurred the Führer's wrath by making an inappropriate remark during the discussion, so Hitler swiftly kicked him out. Needless to say, the atmosphere in the carriage remained rather stormy until Berlin.

Security measures were tightened after the attack, but they had not yet reached the point of searching people's briefcases as they entered headquarters. Since every officer coming 'to report' was carrying a briefcase, it was easy for Count Stauffenberg [Claus von Stauffenberg (1907–44)] to bring a bomb into the meeting room on that memorable morning of 20 July 1944. He placed it against the leg of the table, very close to Hitler, then left the room on the pretext of making a telephone call. It was at that moment the explosion occurred. Several people around Hitler were killed, while he suffered a violent concussion. Both his eardrums were perforated and he also had some bruising from the force with which he was thrown against the table.

At the time, he had invited me to share his meals alone with him, but given the drama that had just unfolded, I was convinced that lunch that day would not take place. However, against all expectations, I was summoned at 3 o'clock in the afternoon. With an anxious heart, I went to meet him, expecting the worst. When I entered his bare room in the bunker, which looked more like a monastic cell than the dining room of the most powerful man in Germany, he rose from his chair with difficulty and gave me his hand with a forced smile. I could tell that his eyes were searching mine, trying to read the look on my face. To my surprise, I admit that his face seemed fresh and calm under the blinding light of the electric bulbs. He told me about his injuries: his right arm was crushed against the table and something heavy had fallen on his kidneys, although he did not know what. He was still surprised at how quickly the drama had unfolded and joked that a bomb attack was an easy way to die.

He then described his personal physician Morell's panic, as he had to bring Hitler to his senses so that he could give him first aid. I was surprised to see that Hitler's hair, which was usually tousled and fell in locks over his forehead, was very well-groomed. I asked if he had had time to call his hairdresser yet, but he took my hand and said, 'Here, touch my hair; it's slightly burned and that's why it's holding up so well.'

With great ease, Hitler then explained to me how the assassination attempt had taken place. At first, he thought a bomb had been thrown in from the outside, through the window. 'I was incredibly lucky,' he told me. 'It was the heavy table leg that the briefcase was placed against which stopped the fragments intended for me. The stenographer sitting next to me, who was taking the minutes of the meeting, had both his legs blown off. I really was incredibly lucky! If the explosion had taken place in the bunker's large room and not in a wooden hut, I'm convinced that everyone there would've been killed. Strangely enough, I'd had a feeling for some time that something extraordinary was going to happen. I felt a danger hanging over me and had already given the order to increase surveillance, do you remember?'

In fact, on 19 July, Hitler had seemed very worried and nervous to me. When I asked him why he was so concerned, he had replied: 'I hope nothing happens to me.' Then, after a heavy silence: 'It'd be the final straw if something bad happened now. I can't afford to fall ill, not when there's no one to replace me in the difficult situation Germany is experiencing.'

Hitler asked me to go to see the meeting room where the explosion had taken place and had what was left of his uniform after the attack brought to me. The trousers were completely torn, with only the belt holding them together. A large piece of fabric had been ripped from the back of his jacket. Hitler considered this uniform a trophy and had it sent to Fräulein Braun at the Berghof, with orders to guard it carefully.

He further described to me how his servants had reacted after the explosion. Linge [Heinz Linge (1913–80)], his valet, was literally foaming with rage, while his other valet, Harndt [Wilem Arndt (1913–45?)], was sobbing with fear.

The Duce's visit was scheduled for the afternoon of 20 July. When I proposed the meeting be postponed until later, I was convinced that Hitler would agree with my suggestion, but, to my surprise, he briskly replied: 'No, there's no question of avoiding him! I have to see him. You'd think foreign propaganda would be only too happy to be able to spread the most infamous lies.'

Immediately after our lunch, Hitler asked the Duce to come to his office. After a short interview, he took him to the hut where the explosion had taken place and explained the events in detail.

In the meantime, the perpetrator of the attack had been

discovered. The telephone operator on duty at the switchboard had noticed that Count von Stauffenberg had gone into the meeting room with a briefcase and had left empty-handed immediately after Hitler's arrival. It was also established that he had not made any telephone calls, but immediately after the explosion had rushed to the airfield, where an aircraft was waiting for him.

When we gathered around Hitler for tea at 5 o'clock, the news of his arrest was brought to us. Hitler was initially furious that von Stauffenberg had reached Berlin, but when he was informed that it was thanks to this fact that all the members of the plot had been arrested, he exclaimed joyfully:

'I've nothing more to fear. This turn of events must be seen as a sign that Germany is now saved. Finally, I have the swine who've been sabotaging my work for years. For months I'd been telling Schmundt [Rudolf Schmundt (1896–1944), his first adjutant and head of the Wehrmacht's central personnel department] about my suspicions, but, with his Parsifal manner, he believed none of it. Now I have proof that the entire General Staff is contaminated. You'll see in the end that the Crown Prince was the instigator of this whole affair.'

The next day, Hitler had the flooring in his office and bedroom torn up to check whether a bomb was hidden there. From then on, every officer who entered his headquarters with a briefcase was subjected to a thorough search.

It was strictly forbidden to leave a briefcase unattended in the same building as him. Also, from this time on, all food intended for Hitler was carefully examined and his medicines were initially analysed in an SS laboratory. In his fury, he also had any gifts sent to him in the form of food destroyed, including caviar (which he was very fond of), pralines, fruit, cakes, etc. Hitler was now in the grip of a veritable psychosis of persecution. To ensure his cook's complete devotion, he showered her with kindness, even going so far as to invite her to our 5 o'clock teas.

However, Hitler's good mood and the happy physical condition he found himself in after the assassination attempt were not to last, and the day after he began to complain of pain in his ears and back. Thanks to his amazing willpower, he managed to keep to his daily schedule until he collapsed on 18 September. He was struck by a particularly acute attack of stomach cramps and had to take to his bed. Jaundice also set in at the same time, meaning he had to stay in bed for three weeks.

In March 1945, rumours spread that a new attack was being prepared and so security measures were tightened further. It was forbidden to enter the park surrounding the Chancellery bunker after 8 o'clock in the evening, and the sentries, equipped with police dogs, were ordered to shoot at any suspicious persons. The doors and windows of the houses in which his guard detachment was stationed, and which bordered the park on the Hermann-Göring-Strasse side, were blocked up. There was now only one access gate left, which was very closely guarded. Visitors were accompanied by the SS when they entered the headquarters, and frequent and unscheduled inspections ensured that no undesirables unduly crossed the threshold.

The assassination attempt of 9 November 1939, which Hitler

had miraculously escaped, had already convinced him definitively of his 'mission', a belief that had also spread to almost all sections of the German population. Indeed, it had grown to such a proportion that, subsequently, confidence in Hitler remained, even in the face of his most resounding failures.

This faith in the Führer had been on the verge of vanishing during the Wehrmacht's disastrous retreat in Russia, but the assassination attempt of 20 July 1944 acted as a stimulant to the people, and Goebbels knew how to use propaganda to exploit this strange event with extraordinary skill. Hitler himself was transformed by it, openly proclaiming himself as the Redeemer of Germany.

However, I do not believe that the majority of the population retained the veneration for him as before; rather, in its despair, it clung to him like a drowning man to a lifeline.

*

Hitler rejected all philosophical concepts that were not based on complete materialism. He proclaimed that man's role ended with his death and allowed himself the most basic puns when speaking of survival in a better afterlife. I have often wondered who, in these conditions, he believed called him to fulfil his mission on earth. Likewise, I never understood why he regularly ended his big speeches with an invocation to the Almighty, and I am convinced he did this only to win the sympathy of the Reich's Christian population. Once again, he was simply playing a terrible game.

Whenever the conversation turned to the spiritual life, he rose up in cynical terms against Christianity, whose dogmas he fought with a filthy violence. His conviction was summed up in this often-repeated phrase: 'Christianity set the world back in its natural development by 2,000 years. Humanity has been scandalously exploited and deprived of its most absolute rights. Faith in a better afterlife has detached man from earthly realities and from the duties he assumes towards humanity from birth.'

He did, however, profess genuine admiration for the religious sisters working as nurses in hospitals, and he often praised them by saying: 'Because they're free from all material interests, they can devote themselves with total dedication to caring for the sick. There are no better nurses than the hospital sisters.'

Hitler was well aware that simple men tied to their daily work instinctively yearn for a form of the supernatural to elevate them above the mundane aspects of their existence. This innate need has been admirably exploited by the Catholic Church, which knew how to attract men by the mystical character of its cult, the marvellous architecture of its cathedrals, the elevation of its sacred music and its majestic rites that unfold in the intoxicating atmosphere of incense. Hitler was an admirer of the organisational genius of Christianity, which had succeeded in building churches of all styles in even the smallest villages, often endowing them with considerable treasures.

He nevertheless found that the Protestant Church gave an impression of poverty in its natural simplicity. At the New Year's party at the Chancellery, the majestic appearance of Nuncio

Pacelli [Eugenio Pacelli (1876–1958), the future Pope Pius XII], who overwhelmed the representatives of the Protestant Church with his extraordinary personality, often served as a comparison between the two tendencies.

'The mysticism of the Catholic Church', said Hitler, 'is admirably suited to the nature of the southern Germans, while Protestantism, with its severe temple lines, adapts itself to the form of northern Christianity.' The Catholic Church, he said, showed remarkable skill in choosing its servants. The priests in the villages are almost all of peasant origin, which creates a powerful and natural bond between them and the population.

Hitler was astute enough to understand that he could not simply remove the moral support that faith provides, and the Party's manifesto stipulated absolute religious freedom for its members. Many Party members never left the Church and remained faithful to their beliefs. Hitler knew that many Germans had made the theatrical gesture of leaving their religion, but had kept their faith intact, which assured them spiritual support during the harsh trials of war. It is known that Bormann led a cynical campaign against the Cross, the symbol of Christianity, in schools and homes, especially in southern Germany. This triggered a genuine revolt for freedom of worship, and, at Hitler's insistence, he had to back down.

XIV

I have no enemies; if I discover any, I will eliminate them.
Himmler

This sentence, pronounced one day by Reichsführer SS Himmler when he was in a good mood, applied not just to him, but to the whole of National Socialist policy. The civilised world was shocked by the gruesome revelations of the concentration camps. And yet there are still honest Germans today who ask themselves the question: how were such atrocities possible? Others are still convinced that these barbaric acts were committed without Hitler's consent or knowledge.

I can say with certainty that Himmler accurately informed Hitler about everything that was happening in the death camps, and he considered all the atrocities as repressions necessary for the stability and development of his regime. However, in this area, as in so many others, he jealously guarded his good reputation and considered it unacceptable that his name could be mixed up with the inhumane acts and deeds that took place in these places. It is in this regard that he undoubtedly played his most hypocritical role and exploited the good faith of a large number of his supporters, with astonishing cynicism.

It is noteworthy that all conversations between Hitler and

Himmler took place one-on-one, behind carefully closed doors. Only Bormann was allowed to attend from time to time.

When Hitler was told during meetings about the rumours circulating concerning mass executions and the cruelties perpetrated in the concentration camps, he avoided answering them and immediately moved on to another subject. I rarely heard him give evasive answers. He would never have admitted to the inhumane harshness of his repressive laws in front of witnesses.

One day, some generals approached Himmler about the cruelties committed in Poland. To my surprise, he recused himself, insisting that he was only carrying out the Führer's orders, before immediately saying: 'The Führer must not be tainted by these facts at any cost; I, Himmler, take full public responsibility for this.'

It is obvious that no member of the Party or SS leader, however influential, would have dared to take such measures without first referring the matter to Hitler. He knew perfectly well that the Gestapo's methods weighed heavily on his people and that they alone allowed him to nip all desires for independence in the bud. Not only did he approve of the inhumane actions committed by his henchmen but was indisputably the inspiration for them. He was also completely insensitive to the procession of pain and hardships that war engendered. The misery and destruction that befell his own people left him cold. How many times did he tell us with a cynical pout: 'Millions of human beings perish from natural disasters without daily life coming to a halt. All the hardships of war and the loss of human life count for nothing in light of historical events.'

Another day, when attention was drawn to the enormous losses the Wehrmacht had suffered among its young officers, Hitler replied without hesitation: 'But isn't that what these young people are here for?'

The blind brutality with which Hitler treated his senior officers is also significant, and it should not be forgotten that all the death sentences for his generals were signed by him personally.

One can imagine the hatred these disciplinary measures might arouse in the Wehrmacht command. I remember the violent reaction to the death sentence for the general who had abandoned the city of Feodosia to the enemy without having received orders to do so. The defenders of Cherbourg and Königsberg also went to the execution post for having yielded to a superior enemy. All these sentences were handed down without any serious investigation into the degree of guilt of those concerned and were all requested by Hitler himself.

In his determination to fight 'until five past twelve', as he was wont to say, he had summary tribunals set up, equipped with a firing squad. These organisations moved behind the engaged troops, pronouncing and carrying out death sentences against officers and men whose only crime had been to doubt German victory. For the record, I will also cite the decree that made an entire family responsible for the treasonous acts committed by one of its members. A terrible arbitrary regime was established in Germany, under the pretext of frightening the doubters. Women, old people and children were arrested, stripped of their property and imprisoned, actions that were a genuine crime against the German people.

Hitler knew no bounds when it came to eliminating people believed to be suspicious or politically compromised. The means by which he got rid of all those who had taken part in the 20 July plot displayed such sadism that one is left confounded by its inhumanity. The fact that generals who until that day had been irreproachable were hanged on hooks like animals for slaughter, not to mention the fact it was all filmed to show to the General Staff as an example, proves that such cruelty, such barbarity, could only be conceived by the unconscious mind of a tyrant.

In conducting the war, Hitler dreamed only of destruction. In his propaganda speeches, terms such as wipe out the cities, reduce the enemy to nothing, etc., etc., constantly reappeared. During the speech he gave us at the Wolfsschanze, on the day the campaign in the West was launched, Hitler mimicked the attitude of Frederick the Great before the Battle of Leuthen and ended it with a grand theatrical gesture, exclaiming: 'The dawn of the last war between Germany and France has just broken, and I will completely destroy our hereditary enemy. I foresee its total annihilation.'

However, a man's true feelings are better manifested in the small actions of daily life than on great occasions. I will cite an incident of which I was a victim, a trivial incident, but one that is well calculated to reveal the cruel rancour of which Hitler was capable.

One evening, during the usual tea, Hitler had once again repeated his favourite theme: the harmful nature of alcohol and nicotine. He made particularly violent reproaches towards the army stewards, who, due to the allocation of cigarette rations, had made 'smokers' out of almost all the soldiers. I explained to him that it was the boredom of long vigils in the trenches or prolonged stays in air-raid shelters that had prompted everyone to smoke more. This suggestion had already earned me one of those disapproving looks that Hitler had perfected, but he continued to explain to us, with examples to support his argument, that the abuse of these two poisons made the mind dull and slow. Seized by a furious desire to contradict him, I replied that Professor H. [*TN*: perhaps Professor Haase?], who indulged heartily in these so-called vices, was nonetheless the most skilful and tactful man in the whole headquarters.

Hitler did not answer me, but I felt that I had overstepped the mark. In the following days, the famous teas were cancelled and, in the few, necessary words we exchanged, Hitler was glacially polite. My remark had seriously injured his pride. When a friend of mine asked him shortly afterwards why the tea sessions were no longer taking place, Hitler, in an irritated tone, replied that an 'old man' could not expect us to sacrifice all our evenings for him. I realised then that my unkind remark had simply offended his vanity.

This incident was the cause of continual trouble to me for many months. I finally decided to apologise to him, but Hitler coldly brushed it aside, remarking ironically that he saw no reason for it. I thus considered the incident closed, but I was wrong. I had practically ceased to exist for him. Outside the office, he systematically avoided me, so all I had to do was adopt the same attitude.

During our trips, I retired very early in the evening to avoid the boredom of the tête-à-têtes, which were equally unpleasant for everyone. One evening, however, he sent his adjutant to order me to join the small group of companions that regularly formed around him. I interpreted this gesture as an indication of reconciliation, but Hitler maintained his intransigent coldness towards me, and this intolerable attitude lasted for another month. The moral torture he inflicted on me revealed all the cruelty he was capable of, just from the slightest annoyance. His punctilious sensitivity never forgave the smallest affront.

Towards the end, his famous outbursts of anger became more and more numerous and violent. In his moments of crisis, he would bang his desk or the walls with his clenched fists, his facial features tensed in a mask of hatred. He then overwhelmed the guilty party, be they a general or a simple officer, with crude epithets, picked from the vocabulary of the local courts. It was as if we were hearing a Prussian sergeant explaining himself to a young recruit. These fits of fury usually ended with these sentences: 'Get out of my sight and consider yourself fired. You're lucky I'm not having you shot on the spot.'

He would then quickly regain control of himself, before pursing his cruel lips, the thinness of which he hid under his little moustache, and dictating to one of his colleagues the punishment the guilty party was to receive. He systematically sought to share the hatred he felt against those who were hostile to him with all those who approached him. Even foreign statesmen were not safe from his furious proselytising. I was always impressed by the arguments he developed when Mussolini or Horthy [Miklós Horthy (1868–1957), regent of the Kingdom of Hungary, 1920–44] tried to make him adopt a more conciliatory attitude towards the Jews. In these moments, Hitler abandoned all formality and depicted the Jewish danger in the most macabre colours before his partners. His long explanations always ended with the conclusion that the Jews had to be eliminated at all costs. He never used a more concise expression, but he always pronounced the word 'eliminate' with such passionate contempt that no one could have any doubt as to its true meaning. He was always in a good mood when he could tell us that foreign visitors had informed him about the racial measures taken in their countries. The day Antonescu [Ion Antonescu (1882–1946), dictator of Romania, 1940–4] announced the 'disappearance' of the Jews in Bessarabia [*TN*: a historical region in eastern Europe, bounded by the River Dniester to the east and the River Prut to the west], Hitler's opinion of him skyrocketed. On the other hand, I saw Hitler remain impassive in the face of Horthy's genial argument preferring to say that, all things considered, it was simply not possible to throw the Jews out into the street or to kill them.

Even in diplomatic conversations, Hitler indulged in violent remarks against his political enemies, never failing to urge his visitors to treat their enemies in the same way he did those in the concentration camps. He did not even hesitate to speak of deportation and repressive measures when referring to the ruling families of Italy, Romania and Yugoslavia. He knew that those circles were hostile to him and had therefore naturally exposed themselves to his hateful vindictiveness.

XV

I have no successor.

Hitler

On 16 February 1945, I was waiting for Hitler in the small room of the Reich Chancellery for our one-on-one lunch. Everything was ready as we waited for the master. The curtains of the dining room, which was located in the right wing of the Radziwill Palace, were completely drawn so as to prevent the Führer of the Third Reich from seeing the state of destruction in the other part of the palace.

Outside, a bright winter sun played on the ruins and rubble, but the lights were on in the room. From time to time, the head waiter came to glance at the table, which was set with great taste and on which, next to Hitler's place setting, the pills he took before and after his meals were lined up in neat little piles. The small glass of 'Pepsin' wine, which he drank during lunch, was also there.

It was not until around 3 o'clock that the maître d' came to me to whisper in my ear that 'the Chief' was arriving. Immediately after this, Hitler entered the room where I was waiting and came towards me, a sullen expression on his face. As he kissed my hand, like normal, his gaze was absent. He was in a state of extreme agitation and began to give vent to his discontent as soon as he sat down at the table:

'I was angry with Albrecht [one of his personal adjutants]. Eva can't see it. I have to watch over everything. I'm being deceived on all sides. I gave the order to close the exit from my bunker onto Voss-Strasse with iron bars. I asked Albrecht if this work had been carried out according to my instructions and he replied in the affirmative. I've just noticed that they only poured concrete on it, which is completely ineffective.

'I can't trust anyone any more. I'm nothing more than a wretched man, betrayed by everyone. It makes me sick. If I didn't have my trusty Morell by my side, I wouldn't be able to complete my work. And to think that those two idiots, doctors Brandt and Hasselbach, wanted me to get rid of him, without asking themselves what'd become of me without his care. If something happened, Germany would be without a Führer, because I have no successor. The first one I had in mind, lost his mind [Hess]. The second one lost all the population's sympathy [Göring]. The third lost the confidence of the Party [Himmler].'

Hitler had launched this tirade in a tone of extreme irritation. Wanting to know his real opinion, when I said to him, cautiously, 'But, my Führer, the people speak a lot of Himmler as having been designated as your successor,' Hitler cried out violently, 'I don't see what you mean. Himmler is a man without any artistic culture.'

I replied that for the time being, the question of fine arts was of no importance and that Himmler always had the possibility, if necessary, of having access to art advisers.

At these words Hitler gave me a furious look and lost all control. 'Don't talk so stupidly! What's wrong with you? As if it were so easy to surround yourself with men of value. I wouldn't have waited for your advice to do it, if I'd the chance.'

I remained stunned by this violence of words and did not breathe another word. Hitler continued to reel off sentences in an interminable monologue, before gradually calming down. When his fury had subsided and he noticed my disapproving silence, he patted me affectionately on the shoulder. 'I agree that we shouldn't talk about politics at the dinner table. I apologise for starting such an unreasonable discussion.'

As he left the table, he stood near me and paused for a few moments. His whole attitude was that of a man who had resigned himself to seeing his work shortly collapse. 'Well, keep looking for who my successor could be. For my part, I keep thinking about the problem, and I can't seem to solve it.'

It was during the incident related above that I first heard Hitler speak of the SS chief with such contempt. Perhaps it was due to the recent collapse of the Vistula front, which Himmler, promoted *in extremis* to commander of the army group, had promised to hold at all costs. Furthermore, he was rarely mentioned during our conversations around the fireside.

When Hitler spoke of Himmler, he praised the SS leader's remarkable care for his men and their families, while also proclaiming that he had absolute confidence in him.

In my opinion, however, he was seriously mistaken on this last point. I had observed the methods Himmler used to fill Hitler's entourage with men who were entirely devoted to him. It was through these manoeuvres that Fegelein, Dr Stumpfeger [*sic.*] and many others had succeeded in occupying important positions with the Führer. I was convinced that Himmler was just waiting for the moment when power would fall into his hands like a ripe fruit.

One day, when Hitler had once again expressed his unlimited confidence in the leader of the black militia, I looked at him with a sceptical smile. The Führer had not failed to notice this and, fixing me with his bewitching eyes, said to me in an almost threatening voice: 'Do you doubt it, perhaps?' I managed to hold his gaze, which had inspired so many people, and did not answer, but I had the distinct impression that Hitler himself could not see clearly what his police chief was doing. The matter was closed.

Himmler was not a social darling, which is why he was rarely invited in small groups to the Berghof. I only remember seeing him at tea parties following important conferences. He and Hitler only ever talked about trivial things in my presence.

Himmler had two hobbies: first, his visits to the front. He always came back with overflowing enthusiasm for the bravery and dedication of his 'boys'. Second, agricultural issues. He had studied agricultural engineering and was passionate about all things to do with the earth. He even encouraged the study of animal husbandry and botany in several research institutes. In one of them, Dr Fahrenkamp produced a poison prepared from lily of the valley and foxgloves, which apparently had the property of making meat edible in a state of putrefaction.

Himmler was very proud of this latest discovery and predicted global success for it.

Hitler rarely discussed racial issues with him. In these cases, Himmler always criticised the un-Aryan appearance of a number of German artists. He did not understand how a regime under the banner of Nordic racism accepted that the physique of certain film actors was a pure negation of the Aryan ideal. They never spoke to me about concentration camps.

Himmler's presence still weighed heavily on society. He created an indefinable atmosphere of fear and unease around him. Next to the Führer, however, Himmler merely gave off the impression of a dull petty bourgeois, despite his hidden power.

After the retreat from the Vistula, his visits to the headquarters became rarer and the favour he had enjoyed with Hitler was definitively ruined.

On the other hand, Hitler retained a soft spot for Göring until the end, despite the terrible disagreements the conduct of the war had caused between them. Hitler liked to talk about Göring. He considered him a faithful and devoted companion and benignly overlooked his insatiable need for luxury, his passion for fancy uniforms, jewels and decorations, saying that such weakness could not make people forget that Göring had been an extraordinary fighter during the First World War and in the period during the struggle for power. Nevertheless, Hitler found it difficult to forgive him for the failures of the Luftwaffe from 1940 onwards, attributing them to the fact that Göring was not a technician and had been betrayed by his colleagues, as he himself was. Hitler blamed the Luftwaffe disasters on Udet's [Ernst Udet (1896–1941)] stubbornness in wasting two years developing a new type of aircraft. To top it all off, the latter turned out to be a complete 'failure'.

In the autumn of 1944, when rumours spread that Göring was clearly losing interest in the air war and was wasting his time on trivialities at his residence at Karinhall [*TN*: Carinhall], Hitler told me: 'Of course, I would've preferred that he not marry that woman. He's completely in love with her and no longer does his job with the necessary heart.'

However, despite the violent altercations between them, Hitler forgave Göring; as far as the latter was concerned, Hitler was all about clemency.

One day he had requisitioned a painting that the antique dealer Haberstock had acquired for Hitler in Paris. Frightened by the consequences such a gesture might bring, Haberstock came to find me so that I could speak to the Führer about it. This I did with all the care that such a mission required. I could not, though, avoid an outburst of anger at the lack of restraint with which Göring had operated. Hitler fumed: 'How dare he go behind my back. I swear he'll grab something as soon as I see it.' Nevertheless, that was the end of it, and Göring kept the painting.

I have already said that towards the end of the war, Hitler no longer considered Göring as his possible successor. He hardly took him seriously any more and did not spare him the harshest of criticisms. Yet despite the loss of prestige Göring had suffered in his eyes, Hitler still had a soft spot for his former comrade in arms. When the approach of enemy aircraft was announced at the end of General Staff meetings, Hitler always had someone call Karinhall to find out whether the Reichsmarschall had returned safely.

All these facts confirm my conviction that it was never Hitler who, on 20 April 1945, ordered the arrest and execution of Göring. The famous telegram could only be the work of Bormann, Hitler's henchman in the last years of the war.

XVI

I never think about it, leaving Berlin; I'd rather kill myself.
Hitler, March 1945

I have no hesitation in stating that Hitler and his companion Eva voluntarily took their own lives. This fateful gesture was not only the final step, consecrating the collapse of Hitler's work, but it also corresponded to the convictions and theories he had professed during the previous three years concerning man's responsibility for his own destiny.

Before the war, he used to say that every individual must bear the consequences of their actions. In his eyes, even the worst ordeals could not justify abandoning the struggle. Hitler sincerely pitied people who were driven to voluntarily leave life in despair and was convinced that a simple piece of advice or a little encouragement in critical moments was enough to restore confidence to a desperate person.

Hitler changed this opinion completely in the last years of the war, especially after the assassination attempt of 20 July 1944. It is curious to note how his mentality was transformed after he had assiduously read the works of the philosopher Schopenhauer. Little by little, he had come to accept the theory that life was not worth living when it held nothing but disillusionment and misery.

During the evenings at his headquarters in East Prussia, Hitler often described to me the state of mind of men who, when faced with the abandonment of their strength, feel themselves slowly dying: 'When a man is nothing more than a living ruin, what's the point of continuing to live? One can no longer speak of cowardice or desertion in the face of duty.'

He often told me of the painful feeling he felt whenever he found himself in the presence of a man in decline, although I do not know whether he fully realised himself how much he had fallen into a state of physical decrepitude, despite his prodigious willpower. During his illness in September 1944, I often visited him in the room he occupied in his small bunker, where not even a ray of sunlight ever penetrated. I saw that Hitler was completely exhausted. In a faint voice, he described the terrible pain his stomach cramps were causing him: 'If these spasms were to continue,' he told me, 'my life would no longer have any meaning. In which case, I wouldn't hesitate to put an end to it.'

These words were spoken in a tone of such helpless despair that I could not help but pity him. I was overcome with emotion at the sight of this exhausted body gripped by atrocious suffering. The atmosphere of the place further accentuated the painful impression I felt in front of the all-powerful master of Germany; the narrow camp bed, the cold, smooth concrete walls, everything oozed the misery of a prison cell. The man himself, his features convulsed, lay before me in his white nightgown edged with blue piping. He already seemed to be breathing the suffocating air of the tomb. From time to time, he still tried to save face by showing a small forced smile. It was no longer the Führer of a Greater Germany before me, just a poor wretch.

Hitler never fully recovered from this crisis. Later, in Berlin, when he found himself lying on the sofa during the nighttime teas, completely exhausted by the efforts of the day, he often confided to me that humanity was too sick for life to be worth living any more. Human duplicity had disappointed him to the extent that he had lost faith in life.

'Animals are more faithful than men,' he repeated. From time to time his gaze would rise to the portrait of Frederick the Great that adorned the wall above his desk, and he would repeat the latter's famous words: 'Ever since I've studied humans, I've loved dogs.'

In January 1945, when Hitler returned from Bad Nauheim to Berlin, he was visibly wasting away and was in an almost permanent state of agitation. His monologues during the tea sessions were nothing more than a monotonous repetition of the same old stories. His repertoire became increasingly restricted, often telling us the same stories at noon and then in the evening. This is what he told us almost day after day: 'Blondi, that wretched pest, came to wake me up again this morning. She came up to my bed with a friendly expression, but when I asked her if she needed to go out, she quickly withdrew to her corner. What a smart dog!' Or again: 'See how much my hand has improved. I don't shake any more; I hardly shake any more.'

It sometimes happened that Hitler would greet someone without realising he had already done so a few moments before;

his memory loss was becoming evident. The topics he still enjoyed discussing became increasingly dull and uninteresting. He no longer spoke about racial issues, economic and political problems, nor did he parade the history of Antiquity before our imaginations, as he had loved to do, while explaining to us in his own way the causes of the collapse of the Roman Empire. He who had once been passionately interested in all biological issues, in botany and zoology, in the social evolution of humanity (he was convinced that the latter would one day be replaced by a termite state), now in recent months only talked about dog breeding, food supplies and the stupidity and wickedness of men. He had become absolutely disconcerting in his judgements of those around him. People who had enjoyed his special favours for many years suddenly lost all consideration in his eyes, and without justification.

At the table, he increasingly insisted on unappetising conversations. When he met a woman during the day whose lipstick was too flashy for his taste, he did not hesitate to explain, during the meal, that the lipsticks were made from Parisian sewage.

He also happened to tell us a theory about his own blood, describing with sadistic pleasure how he had regularly used leeches to reduce his blood pressure. When one day I pointed out to him how disgusting I found those filthy beasts, he replied, quite astonished: 'But they're nice little creatures that do a lot of good work.' However, he did go on to tell us how Morell was now taking blood samples from him, a process he found more convenient and cleaner.

When he was in a bad mood and saw us eating meat or even

just improving boiled vegetables with a little meat juice, he would sometimes say to us, referring to the blood samples Morell was taking from him: 'I fully intend to make you some black pudding with my excess blood. Why not? Since you love meat so much?'

When he first made this remark to us, we were absolutely appalled and did not hesitate to show him the complete disgust he could inspire in us at the table. But it was a bad move for us, because instead of changing the subject, he insisted on giving us a whole lesson to prove to us that blood was very appetising. I also noted with horror that Hitler had gradually lost all the scrupulous reserve he had always displayed in the presence of his female staff. In the twelve years I had spent at his side, he had never allowed himself the slightest derogatory remark, the slightest liberty, the slightest swear word. During the last months in Berlin, he had shed all feelings of modesty. One morning, a friend, whose extravagant attire he had always appreciated, arrived in the bunker of the Chancellery during an alert wearing musketeer gloves and an immense hat with a turned-up brim, all the colour of wine dregs. Hitler stood before her and admiringly suggested that her beauty would not suffer if she wore only a hat and gloves, and laughingly invited her to come to the bunker dressed like that from now on. This tasteless joke was repeated several times.

The intramuscular injections Morell regularly administered had a visibly stimulating effect on Hitler. Each time he experienced the benefits of Morell's syringe, his demeanour afterwards was more relaxed and his conversation became freer. Once, as he lay before us on the sofa for tea at dawn, he began to stretch his whole body and stiffen his arms, with an indistinct grunt. He then looked at us strangely and explained that through these simple gestures, a man can get along with his partner. We were frozen with shock.

After this incident, I asked Dr Morell what exactly was going on with Hitler and whether he ever gave him aphrodisiacs. Morell replied: 'Yes, I'm now giving him new hormones to boost his strength.'

Yet Hitler's decline had taken on such proportions in those final days that I could not help wondering whether we were not simply dealing with a mentally unbalanced person. The most contradictory rumours had begun circulating on this subject. More and more people claimed that Hitler had gradually lost some of his faculties, especially since the failed assassination attempt of 20 July 1944. Everything was discussed in hushed tones, as the slightest indiscretion would have meant immediate death to the imprudent person who blasphemed the idol of the Third Reich. But the idea haunted me. Using all the circumspection I was capable of, every time I alluded to this to Dr Morell or to the generals around him, I was treated as if I was mad myself. It was agreed that Hitler was living more and more on the fringes of reality, but that he still followed the development of events with lucidity. He was fully aware of the race to the abyss in which his Reich was engaged, but his boundless stubbornness and faith in his mission prevented him from drawing the necessary conclusions. He still harboured the insane hope that he would be able to turn the situation around and snatch victory at the finish line, and announced before the German people that this change would take place on a political level.

In his last address to the Gauleiters, on 26 February 1945, he had expressed his unwavering conviction that German diplomacy would succeed in breaking up the Allies' united front. A few days later, during a conference with his military experts, he gave them a glimpse of something 'new' via the use of the famous secret weapons. He kept repeating: 'Be patient, we have to buy time.'

This explains his intention to transform the Bavarian Alps into a powerful natural fortress. However, when I learned that he had sent boys from Berlin's Hitler Youth against the Russian tanks, whose circle of iron surrounded the capital, I could no longer shake off the idea that such actions could only be the work of a mentally irresponsible person. Such horrors could not emanate from a man in full possession of his faculties.

It was necessary to establish the extent to which Hitler's dementia was advanced, but only an experienced psychiatrist, living in his wake, could have determined this. I spoke with men who had the opportunity to talk with him during meetings, shortly before the fall of the capital. Despite the overwhelming ordeals of the time, these generals and senior officials had managed to maintain complete lucidity. Every time they left the meeting room, they were literally devastated and confided to me in half-sentences their belief that Hitler had certainly lost control of his actions long ago. These confessions confirmed my own convictions.

From that moment on, I felt a chill down my spine every time he surprised me with his oddities. The thought that the German people were at the complete mercy of his ramblings overwhelmed me, and it became a genuine obsession of mine to know the precise limits of his psychological decline. I could no longer confide my worries to Hitler's entourage. That would have been suicide.

As chance would have it, one day I privately met a former president of the State Court, whom I had known when he worked very closely in the legislative field with Reichsleiter Bormann. Very carefully, I raised with him the question of whether it was possible that Hitler was no longer in possession of all his mental faculties. The answer truly blew me away. This man of character, an eminent and objective jurist, for whom events had in no way affected his unanimously recognised psychoanalytic abilities, answered me with the following sentence, which cut the question with the rigour of a guillotine blade: 'Yes. Hitler has dementia.'

I had further confirmation of this when I stayed at the Berghof for the last time, in April 1945. I had found in Dr Karl Brandt's belongings a press release in which it was announced that the disappearance of a famous psychiatrist from the University of Königsberg had caused concern among the German people. This specialist, whose name escapes me, had been secretly summoned to Hitler's headquarters to examine him, and had concluded that a prolonged stay in a special sanatorium was necessary. He was afterwards immediately summoned by Himmler and then mysteriously disappeared.

Further confirmation was then given to me by Göring himself. A few days before leaving Berlin, he had asked Bormann to give him meeting reports from the last few months. He explained his request by saying he feared they would later be made public and that the German people would learn they had been led by a madman for the last two years. Göring added that this was the only explanation for the incredible insults Hitler had directed at him.

Unfortunately, I cannot judge how far one can believe this statement by Göring. Did he want to destroy these reports in order to erase all traces of his guilt, or did he simply want to hide Hitler's decline? I had the impression that both motives were in play at the same time.

On the evening of 20 April 1945, Hitler called me into his office, along with one of my colleagues. He greeted us with his usual enthusiasm and then said sadly: 'The situation has evolved in the last two weeks in such a way that I'm obliged to disperse my General Staff even more. Pack your things immediately. The car leaves for the south in an hour. You will receive further instructions from Reichsleiter Bormann.'

My colleague and I then asked him if we could stay with him in Berlin. He rejected our offer on the basis that he intended to organise a resistance movement in Bavaria, which he would later join. 'I still need you both,' he said. 'I want to know you're safe. If things become worse, the other two secretaries will also leave Berlin. If any of your young colleagues were to perish in this attempt, it will be down to fate.' Then he dismissed us with these words: 'We'll see each other again soon; I'll join you as soon as possible.'

Hitler had said these words in one breath. He stood before us, his back hunched, his arms dangling, his hair completely white. He tried in vain to hide the trembling in his hand. His eyes, lifeless and tired, were fixed on an imaginary spot. Only a small, tired smile still lit up his hollow features. The disillusioned smile of a completely broken man who had lost all hope.

Shortly afterwards, Hitler called me twice more on the telephone. On the first call, he told me: 'My children, the situation has changed. The circle around Berlin has closed. The car will no longer get through. You'll leave Berlin by plane tomorrow morning.'

Immediately afterwards, his broken voice whispered to me: 'The plane will leave around 2 o'clock, as soon as the alert ends. You must make sure you take off.'

Then his voice changed to a strange gurgle. I asked him to repeat his last words, but he did not answer. He had not hung up the telephone, but all I could hear was a muffled voice that struck my ears like the distant murmur of nothingness.

NOTES

Editor's Note

1 From Librairie Arthème Fayard, 1952.

Chapter I

1 The Wolf's Lair.

Chapter II

1 Deutsches Nachrichtenbüro: the press agency created in 1934 that was under the control of the Nazis.

Chapter VII

1 Widow of a famous piano manufacturer.

Chapter IX

1 Sly dog, clever fox.

Chapter XII

1 Free corps of volunteers created by Himmler in August 1944.

FRIEDRICH SANDER

BLOOD, DUST AND SNOW

DIARIES OF A PANZER COMMANDER IN GERMANY AND ON THE EASTERN FRONT

ARNOLD DÖRING

LUFTWAFFE BOMBER TO NIGHTFIGHTER

THE MEMOIRS OF A KNIGHT'S CROSS PILOT

VOLUME I

EDITED & ANNOTATED BY
THOMAS BAUMERT

FOREWORD BY
JAMES HOLLAND

ARNOLD DÖRING

LUFTWAFFE BOMBER TO NIGHTFIGHTER

THE MEMOIRS OF A KNIGHT'S CROSS PILOT

VOLUME II

FOREWORD BY
RICHARD
OVERY

EDITED & ANNOTATED BY
THOMAS
BAUMERT